MW01628798

JOEY'S ITALIAN

Enjoy!
Joey

JOEY'S ITALIAN

Favorite Recipes from Central New York's
Celebrated Restaurant

Joey DeCuffa
with Denise Owen Harrigan
Photography by James Scherzi
Design by Holly Boice Scherzi

Foreword by Alec Baldwin

DeCuffa Publishing ❧ Syracuse, New York

DeCuffa Publishing
6594 Thompson Road North
Syracuse, New York 13206
www.joeysitalianrestaurant.com

Jacket and book design by Holly Boice Scherzi www.hollyscherzi.com

Library of congress Cataloging-in-Publication Data
DeCuffa, Joey.
Joey's Italian : Favorite Recipes from Central New York's Celebrated Restaurant

Recipes for the home kitchen from Central New York's signature Italian restaurant / by Joey DeCuffa with Denise Owen Harrigan; photography by James Scherzi.
p. cm.
Includes Index.
ISBN: 978-0-615-21887-8 (hardcover)
1. Italian cookery. 2. Joey's (Restaurant)
I. Harrigan, Denise. II. Title.

First printing, 2008

Printed by Monroe Litho, a Forest Stewardship Council certified printer and an EPA Green Power Partner, operating on 100 percent renewable, nonpolluting wind power.

1 2 3 4 5 6 7 8 9 10 | 13 12 11 10 09

This book is lovingly dedicated to

My mom and dad, Eunice and Anthony
Thanks for being who you were, which helped make me who I am today

My wife, best friend and inspiration, Janice

My wonderful daughter, Aletea

My brothers and sister and their families:
Michael and his kids: Dylan, Dakota, Miranda, and Mychailla
Mark and Jackie and their kids: Markie and Toni
Tony and Kelly
Rick
Sharon and Gary Locke
Gary, rest in peace, you will be missed, but will always be in our hearts

My Stepson, Jarrett Colan

Jesse and Courtney Colan, and of course my grandson, Damien aka "the Pissant"

Janice's parents, Warren and Yuki Stone

Diesel my canine companion and loyal taste tester

Marty, Beverly and Dev Quinn

Cousin Ernie and Estelle Caruso

Kevin and Michelle Locke and their daughter Kierstan

My gratitude and appreciation to Aunt Nancy, Aunt Jean and Uncle Chuck and their families

And to my entire extended family thank you for your love and support

Acknowledgments

The years go flying by! Joey's has been open now for twenty-five plus years, that's over nine thousand days serving food and hospitality to more guests than I can count—much less remember all of their names! I would like to thank each and every person that has given me the opportunity to serve them, but there is not enough room here to name them all, so if I missed listing you here, tell me about it the next time you come in!

Rick and Elaine Alesia
The Grimaldi Family—Freddy Grimaldi-Sr. and Jr., Ray Grimaldi
Angelina—my pasta making inspiration from Grimaldi's
Skip Henning
Mr D and Steve aka "Gus" Bocino
Tony Danible and Family
Special thanks to the entire Baldwin family and the Carol Baldwin Foundation—especially Carol, Beth, Alec, Danny, Billy and Stephen Baldwin
Jim and Julie Boeheim
Dick and Sandra McPherson
Dr. Cincota and Joan Cincota
Marty Ventre
John Ventre
Mickey Rooney
Billy "Huge" Fuccillo
Tony and Sherri Giata
Dick and Bonnie Scolaro
John Fogerty
Pineapple and Susie Proctor
Jim and Charlene Tyler
Paul and Sandy Carey
Judge Greenwood
Judge Jim Tormey
Judge John Centro
Marty and Beverley Quinn
D.A. Bill Fitzpatrick
D.A. Glen Suddaby
Ernie and Estelle Caruso
Roy Bernardi
Mike Allen
All the folks at the U.A.W. and the Teamsters Union
John McDougal
Pat and Chris Barrett and family
Joe Riccelli
Frank Magari
John Scuderi
The "Boys" Angelo Pavone and Dino Centra
Jim Parmeli, "Doc" Merola
The "Chi-Chi's"
JPW Riggers
Mayor Matt Driscoll
Nick Pirro
Mike and Sue Bragman
Tony and Mike Santoro
Jack Chaney
Jeff Lewis and the staff at WYNIT
Terry Green

Paula and Bill Knapp
John Femia
John Sucopani
Sam Lanzafame
Dave Olek, Chris Bevans and the staff at Velocitel
John Abdo
Peter Lowe
Bud and Lee Ridley
Mike, Tim, John and our friends at PPC
The Fabrizio family
Ravi
Dr. and Mrs. Gold
Chappy Romano
Ed Dipple
Mark Cavallaro
Nick Petrocello
John Kinsella
The Grenga family
Tom and Jeanie Prinzi
Father Stirpe
Joe Corapi
Our customers from M&T Bank
Dave and Laurie
Dr. Bonavita and his staff
Ralph Stipello
The Mento family
Jeff and Suzanne Difulio
Angelo and Pat
Lesa and Christine from Kemper Insurance
All of our "boating buddies" from the 1000 Islands
Milton Cat and family
Jim Pippins and family
Al and Lydia Davendorf
Lou and Darlene Lattora
"Mootz" and his family
Chet and "Say"
Dickie and Billie, may she rest in peace
Vinnie and Francesca Pagano
Dick and Annette Bruntrager
Ed Childs
Joe and Karen Grosso and family
JMG Builders
Tony D and family
The Nasto family
Mike and Julie Chavoustie
Julie Nestico, rest in peace
Dody and Dean Vlassis
Irv Berliner

All the purveyors that supply us with the ingredients for great food and service: *Mento's Produce, Sysco, Paul DeLima Coffee, Casa Imports, Ventre Packing, Renzi Food Products, Maines, Empire Merchants, Southern Wine and Spirits, Robinson & Smith, Dumac, Andy's Produce, Cousin's Seafood, Community Bakery*

The staff at Joey's, Pronto Joey's and the T.I. Club, *with special thanks to*

Jonathan Blok, aka JB
Rick Zaborny
Belinda Larca
Tammy Collins
Marie Cassella
Milt Ebersole
Linda Volmer
Kathy Bahn
Denny Hayes
Rick DeCuffa
Eddie Rapone

***Special thanks to* The Joey's Cookbook Team**

Jim Scherzi, Scherzi Studios
Holly Scherzi, Holly Scherzi Design
Denise Owen Harrigan
Janice DeCuffa
Kathy Bahn

Recipe Testers

Erin Harrigan
Lorrie Smith

Table of Contents

Foreword

Restaurants. Wow. I mean . . . man. I must have spent a million dollars in restaurants. And of course, you can probably trace that to the fact that, when I was a kid, we never went to a restaurant. Sure, we went to Howard Johnson's All-You-Can-Eat Fish Fry. Or for the chicken. My father had six kids. Four sons. And on a teacher's salary. My relationship to restaurants really began when, what else, I worked in one.

I was a busboy at a local diner in high school. I worked in restaurants in Washington, DC, and New York during college. Some pretty nice places. Some not so nice. You learn a lot about restaurants when you work in one. Not only about people, but about food and service. When I started working in the movie business and, all of the sudden, I could eat in any restaurant I wanted, things began to change. The quality of the food was now viewed on par with decor, ambience, service, wine, not to mention the kind of crowd that ate there. Restaurants became about image, sometimes at the cost of a good meal. I sat in restaurants from Long Island to London, Venice to Paris, Tokyo all the way back to Manhattan, and would sometimes think, "I wish I'd grabbed a slice before dinner." The food was good, but something was missing.

Soon, going out to eat was a drag. The crowds, the parking, the noise, the attitude. Too much bother. I would rather eat at home. In order to enjoy myself in a restaurant, it needed to be like home. I wanted to eat what I wanted, the way I wanted and I wanted to be left alone to enjoy the people I was with. Too much attention by the staff can kill a good restaurant meal. There is a strong sense of timing required. A good restaurant meal is certainly about good food in a comfortable and handsome room. But it's got to flow . . . just right. You walk in and it all begins. And you can't learn that. You either have that in your dining room and kitchen, or you don't. It's like magic. And Joey DeCuffa has got it. Believe me.

Joey's in Syracuse is the dining room for the Italian side of my family. (That's a joke. We are not Italian.) We drive a bit to get there, but it is well worth it. In Joey's, the magic happens from the moment you sit down and lasts until you get up to leave. I can't sit in most restaurants more than ninety minutes. At Joey's, I could sit for three hours. And, yes, ultimately it is about the food. The food at Joey's? Madonn'! You will love it.

Remember . . . if, in the end, you buy this book and you discover you can't cook like Joey DeCuffa, don't worry about it. The answer is Joey's restaurant, off Carrier Circle, in Syracuse, New York.

Alec Baldwin
Actor and Author
Fall 2008

My Story

They tell me I had a very rough childhood. That's not how I remember it. Sure, it was chaotic, growing up in a family with six kids. And sure, my mother was always working—sometimes two jobs at a time—but that's to be expected of a young widow with a brood to feed. But a rough childhood? How rough could it have been, with a pot of my mother's tomato sauce simmering on the stove and a bowl of meatballs sitting on the counter? (The bowl was my mother's solution to the meatball snatchers who raided her sauce as they raced through the kitchen.)

As I look back, there was always something cooking—or baking. My father, Anthony DeCuffa, was a popular Utica baker who died when I was 5 years old. But in his short life, my father made some very smart choices, chief of which was to marry my beautiful Irish-English mother. They met after World War II, when my father—a hard worker and a real go-getter—moved the family bakery next door to Grimaldi's, a small Italian restaurant in Utica, New York. Grimaldi's only waitress was my mother, Eunice Wicks. My father was a daily customer and a big tipper. The rest is history. Anthony and Eunice married and moved to nearby New Hartford. In short order, they had six kids: Sharon, Tony, me, Mark and Michael (the twins), and Ricky, the baby.

As a young bride, my mother learned the fine art of Italian cooking from my father's sisters. My mother was eager to learn, and her sauce was soon considered the best in the DeCuffa family. My father's life also revolved around food. As a mess sergeant in the U.S. Army, he had a hand in developing C-rations. According to family legend, he also created the half-moon or black and white cookie. But when I was a kid, I thought my father was a little crazy, getting up at 3 a.m. to make doughnuts. I remember climbing into the bakery truck to deliver day-old doughnuts to the migrant workers outside town. We would bump down the dirt roads through the pea camps (or corn camps, depending on the season). The workers would come running out of the fields and jump right onto the truck. The doughnuts made those people happy. Making and sharing the doughnuts made my father happy. This connection between people, food and sharing has stayed with me as an influence in how I run my restaurant.

My father was only 42 when he died of a heart attack. I was 5 years old and we had just moved to a big house in the country in the middle of an orchard. I was climbing an apple tree that day, and he was standing beneath it, holding one of the twins in each arm. In those days, there was no 911. My father died before he reached the hospital. Because my mother had twins under the age of 5 and a new baby to cope with, the rest of us kids were split up for a few years. I was sent to a farm, where I did chores from sunrise to sunset, which turned out to be good training for the restaurant business. But before long, we were all back together. Of course my mother always had to work—to this day, my sister, Sharon, still thinks she's our babysitter. My mother spent a few years as a carhop at Kewpee's, home of Utica's best burgers, but eventually she went back to work at Grimaldi's, making the long commute to their new location in Syracuse.

By the age of 12, I was working myself, first in a body shop, then flipping burgers at Kewpee's. Like my father, I was a hard worker, except at school. I often stayed home "sick" but cleaned the house, so what could my mother say? At 16, I dropped out of school and hitchhiked to San Francisco with friends (Hey, these were the sixties!). After four months of panhandling in Berkeley, I went back to New Hartford, where my shoulder-length hair landed me in jail on a loitering charge. After a few days in the tank and a jailhouse crew cut, I was dragged to Grimaldi's by my mother. Freddie Grimaldi Sr. looked me up and down and said, "Wow, what a nice, clean-cut kid." He had known my father, who really was a nice, clean-cut kid.

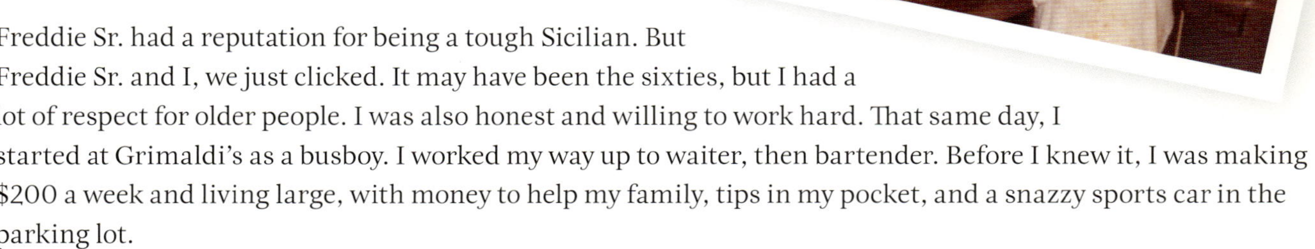

Freddie Sr. had a reputation for being a tough Sicilian. But Freddie Sr. and I, we just clicked. It may have been the sixties, but I had a lot of respect for older people. I was also honest and willing to work hard. That same day, I started at Grimaldi's as a busboy. I worked my way up to waiter, then bartender. Before I knew it, I was making $200 a week and living large, with money to help my family, tips in my pocket, and a snazzy sports car in the parking lot.

I learned the art of waiting on tables from my mother, who made customers feel like the guests of honor and part of the family. I also loved taking care of customers. Then one night, in Grimaldi's back kitchen, I discovered Angelina, an Italian grandmother who spoke very little English and made heavenly pasta, by hand. I was mesmerized by her rhythmic kneading, rolling, cutting, filling, crimping—fettuccine, ravioli, tortellini, manicotti. As a kid, I had watched my aunts make ravioli in their basement kitchens (Does anyone know an Italian family without a kitchen in the basement or a garden out back?) Until I met Angelina, I never considered cooking as a profession. Soon I was finding excuses to go back and watch her work. Then I was punching out after my shift and heading back to help, instead of heading out for a night on the town.

Making pasta with Angelina, my mind stopped racing, and I was totally focused. When I finally made the big decision to work in Grimaldi's kitchen—at a big cut in pay—people thought I was crazy. But from the moment I stepped behind that stove, with the heat and the hollering and everything happening at once, I knew I was home.

Home, maybe, but clueless about cooking. In Grimaldi's kitchen, there were no recipes. No one had the time or inclination to teach me, and it was clearly not macho to ask for help. I learned to cook by imitating the cooks on the line at Grimaldi's. Gradually, the pots and pans became extensions of my hands. I never measured ingredients—also not macho—and I rarely used spoons or spatulas. I'd just grab those panhandles and shake, swirl and flip away.

Even when the heat was really on, with all the burners blazing and orders clipped down the line as far as I could see, the stove was my sanctuary, and my stage. But I was never center stage. This was long before the era of the celebrity chef. The head cook was just one of the crew. There was always more to learn. Grimaldi's was a big operation, with hundreds of guests daily and a reputation as the best Italian restaurant in Central New York.

For the next 14 years, I was the eager apprentice, mastering my craft and absorbing every aspect of this crazy business. By the early 1980s, I was head chef, general manager, and part of the Grimaldi family. Freddie Sr. felt like a father to me. Every night, at the end of my long shift, I drove him home then went back to close the restaurant.

At this point in Grimaldi's history, Freddie Grimaldi Jr. and his brother, Raymond, worked with their father. Sometimes their old-school and new-school ways collided, and I was caught in the middle. One day, Raymond, the restaurant's accountant, told me to control food costs by cutting the pork chops two-inches instead of three-inches thick.

Freddie Sr. saw what I was doing and went ballistic. He picked up the pork chops and threw them at me. It was a turning point in my life. I couldn't win. I realized that I had reached a dead end at Grimaldi's. I had learned a trade, and now it was time to turn that trade into a business. I knew it was the right thing to do, but I felt sick about it. Every day for 14 years, I had lived and breathed Grimaldi's restaurant. And the Grimaldis had treated me like family.

Freddie Jr. eased my guilt when he blessed my departure. "Go do your own thing," he said. "You'll never be who you want to be working for someone else." It must have been predestined. The next day, I ran into a guy who had just closed his Italian restaurant on Carrier Circle in Syracuse. We started talking, and soon we were hatching plans to open Joey's in its place.

I'd be lying if I said I wasn't a little scared. I was 29 years old and a single dad, with a beautiful 3-year-old daughter, Aletea. I had no illusions about the restaurant business. Freddie Grimaldi Jr. had warned me that a good cook is no guarantee of a good restaurant. I knew at that time, two out of three restaurants would go under in their first year, and only eight percent survived beyond five years.

On the other hand, I was willing to work hard. And a voice in my head kept insisting, "Joey, get out there and make something of yourself."

Before we opened Joey's, I enlisted my entire family. The kitchen was coated with grease. Your feet stuck to the floor. For the first week, we scrubbed. Then we painted. We still had a gas station attached to the building—and a jukebox and Pac Man game in the dining room—but I insisted on nice linens. Joey's was not going to be just another spaghetti house. The setting might be slightly makeshift, at first, but the food and service would be first-class. From day one, I was determined to serve classic Italian-American food, made from scratch, with only the best ingredients.

On opening night—November 11, 1982—Joey's was packed. Our eight-burner stove had only three working burners, but we were a hit, right off the bat. Most of our early customers were Grimaldi's regulars who knew good food. They came, they ate, and they came back, with family and friends.

From day one, Joey's felt like home to me. Next to me at the stove was my brother, Mark. Out front, warming up the crowds, was my brother Rick—a born maitre'd. In the back kitchen was my sister-in-law Paula, entrusted with making our signature fresh pasta. And then there was my mother, who left Grimaldi's—supposedly to work for me but really to keep an eye on her tomato sauce, the foundation of our menu. She was always stopping to stir it, taste it, add a dash of this or that.

It would be an understatement to say that my mother spoiled our customers, often at my expense. She never charged for wine refills or for the expensive, imported blue cheese she heaped on the salads (which explains why her regulars were so willing to wait until my mother had an open table). Sometimes I wondered if she were working with me or against me. When I hollered at someone in the kitchen, she'd take them aside and say, "He's crazy, pay no attention to him." At the end of the night, when girls in the bar approached me, my mother would step in and say, "I'm sorry girls. He needs his rest. Joey has a business to run."

My mother was right. I had lot to learn about the business side of the restaurant business. Thank god I didn't know what I didn't know, in those early days. I had learned basic bookkeeping from Freddie Sr.'s wife, Rita, who was like a second mother to me. Rita approached accounting with the same reverence my mother brought to cooking. I now understand why accounting is so important. You have to face your numbers, every day: what you're spending, what you're charging, what you have or don't have at the end of the week.

By facing the numbers yet refusing to compromise on food or service, Joey's earned a great reputation. Carrier Circle, wasn't the hub it is today, and there were predictions that Joey's would be packed at lunch but almost empty at dinner. Not so. Day and night, the locals came. The business crowd and the travelers came, and eventually all the visiting celebrities, professional athletes, politicians, and presidents.

Most important to me, the local Italians came to Joey's. They often said my food was "almost" as good as their mothers'. I was honored. For an Italian, that is the highest compliment.

But I wasn't making a profit. For years, every dime I made went back into the business. I'd choose a new carpet for Joey's over a new car for Joey, a new ice machine over a winter vacation. By 1985, I was feeling more confident, and I converted our upstairs banquet room into a "polished casual" trattoria, decorated like an Italian grocery store. We named it Pronto Joey's and served great pizza, pasta, salads, and sandwiches.

People said I was crazy to compete with myself. But in New York City, I'd seen two great restaurants thrive under one roof. We made that our motto—"Two Great Restaurants Under One Roof"—and Pronto Joey's took right off. My only regret is that my mom didn't get to see the second restaurant succeed. She would have loved Pronto Joey's. Mom passed away in 1987, but in so many ways she is present every day in the restaurant. To this day, I cannot walk by a pot of sauce without stopping to stir it and taste it, just like Mom. If I thought the Vatican would take me seriously, I would have my mother designated as the Patron Saint of Pasta Sauce!

Before long, I felt Pronto Joey's had the potential to become a chain. I opened a second branch in nearby Liverpool. In the old Howard Johnson's on Carrier Circle, I opened an upscale, old-fashioned diner. By then, the circle was booming with new businesses and hotels. During the next 10 years, I invested in seven other restaurants across the country. All the concepts were good, and the food was first-rate. But I was spread too thin. I finally had to face the fact that I'm a micromanager, not a multi-unit operator. I'd rather have one great restaurant than a dozen decent restaurants. I decided to concentrate on the original Joey's and Pronto Joey's. But just as we were ready to downsize, Joey's literally went up in flames. On October 14, 1995, a fire started in the kitchen and raced through the building. Everything was scorched, soaked, or smoke-damaged.

The next day, I stood in the parking lot, ready to give up. Next to me stood Janice, who was then my girlfriend and is now my wife. She was staring at the same smoldering ruins, but she saw the situation differently. I saw the fire as the end of Joey's. Janice saw it as a fresh beginning.

Each time we went back to inspect the damage, I focused on how much water remained on the floor. Janice focused on how much the water had receded. She was teaching me to take a negative and turn it into a positive.

Three days after the fire, Janice threw a surprise birthday party for me. My entire staff turned out, and—with Janice leading the cheer—we stood in a huddle, chanting, "We're coming back, and we're coming back stronger." I realized we could replace everything, except my team. I fought with the insurance company to pay my entire staff—75 people—while we made our comeback. The insurance company said I could only keep my "key" people. I argued that every member of my staff was key. I won. Joey's entire staff came to work everyday. We hauled out debris, then scrubbed, rebuilt, painted, and reupholstered.

Four months later, we reopened. Business went right back through the roof. Thanks to Janice's organizational and motivational skills, we were back, and we were stronger than ever.

But we still had work to do, according to Janice, who worked at the time for a Fortune 500 company. She convinced me that my management style also needed a makeover. From the customer's perspective, our operation looked pretty seamless. But behind the scenes, things could get pretty heated. (Although not as heated as in the early days, when I once tried to dunk my brother Mark's head in a pot of tomato sauce. My mother, as usual, came to his rescue.)

By the time I met Janice, Joey's had grown from a family-style venture into a full-fledged company. We needed more structure—and less hollering. Janice introduced us to mission statements, timelines, and agendas. My staff loved it. I think most people crave structure and strong leadership. The focus of our weekly management meetings changed from venting to planning. Every manager was asked to bring one new idea to the table, then make it happen. Success, I've learned, is 10 percent ideas and 90 percent follow-through. This is what I call my "10-90 rule". Thanks to Janice, we holler less and accomplish a lot more. And I can't remember the last time I threw an ashtray at my brother!

Anyone in the restaurant business will tell you that it's the ultimate team sport. You are only as good as your crew. On average, my employees have worked here for 10 years. Some have been here almost since we opened.

My staff is very loyal to me, and I am very loyal to them. I'm not a corporate suit. When we're busy, I'm on the line cooking beside them. When the kitchen floor is dirty, and I'm the first to arrive, I start my day with a mop in my hand. I'd never ask my staff to do what I wouldn't do myself. My staff is the best in the world. They can sometimes be a pain in the neck, but they're there when I need them, and I'm there when they need me. Which of course makes us family.

On the subject of family: I am delighted that my daughter, Aletea, now works with me at Joey's. During the past five years, she has been learning every angle of this crazy business—much like I did during my priceless apprenticeship at Grimaldi's. I'm proud to say that Aletea has all the right ingredients—the passion, the knowledge, the work ethic—to one day continue the Joey's tradition.

Aletea

I am wrapping up this book just a few days shy of Joey's 25th anniversary, so I'm feeling pretty sentimental—about my staff, my great customers, my wife, my daughter, my restaurant and my family. And especially about my mother and father, Eunice and Anthony DeCuffa, who taught me to love—and to share—great food.

I am grateful to you all.

Joey

Weekly managers meeting at Joey's

Cooking, According to Joey

1 *Buy, grow, beg, or borrow the very best ingredients.* I am convinced that the key to Italian cuisine lies in the quality of ingredients—what you bring into the kitchen is more important than what you do in the kitchen.

2 *Buy in season whenever possible.* Fresh fruit and vegetables are available to us from all around the world. But just because it's available doesn't mean it's flavorful. Grapes imported from Chile in January are every bit as good as grapes from California in June, but a cantaloupe picked ultra green in Central America in March will never have the sweet taste of summer like a locally grown melon in July.

3 *Buy local, whenever possible.* Supermarkets have become wonderful sources for ingredients, but don't forget local farmer's markets and farm stands that dot our country roads. On average, food in America travels 1,500 miles from its original source to your plate, and it doesn't get any tastier or more nutritious along the way.

4 *When you do buy imported products, treat yourself to the good stuff.* This is especially true with traditional Italian ingredients like prosciutto de Parma, Parmigiano-Reggiano, balsamic vinegar, San Marzano tomatoes and olive oil. The Italians are artists when it comes to preserving foods, to the point where it's actually illegal to claim that something is authentic if it hasn't been produced in the prescribed manner. Seek out these superior products, and you'll taste the difference.

5 *Learn to boil water.* Seriously! It matters, especially with pasta. See page 102.

6 *Don't be afraid of onions and garlic, fresh of course.* Peel 'em, chop 'em, sweat 'em, then sauté slowly, in a little olive oil, to release their wonderful flavors. These two ingredients contribute the lion's share of flavor in the Italian kitchen. I have to chuckle when I see a package of pre-chopped onions or a jar of minced garlic in the supermarket. How much time does it take to peel and chop an onion or smash a little garlic? Trust me, what you save in time, you lose in taste.

7 *Make friends with your butcher, fishmonger, and cheese supplier.* They know their stuff and are flattered when you share their passion and seek their advice. They will always be happy to fill special orders for you.

8 *Cook with—not just for—your family and friends.* Italians consider cooking a family affair and a treasured (though not necessarily always a peaceful) tradition. Pass it on. Someday, your kids will cook with their kids . . . and they'll get really sentimental about their memories of cooking with you.

9 *Keep it simple.* The beauty of Italian cooking is that it's not that complicated. When I was in Tuscany, I was asked to cook for a group of "locals" and guests that included a very elegant surgeon who grew up in Florence, lived in New York, and had eaten in the world's finest restaurants. That night I served a simple dinner of roast pork with roasted potatoes. We had a great meal, and we all had a great time, including yours truly because I didn't have to spend the whole night in the kitchen.

10 *Find the fun in cooking.* It's not just a means to an end. The Food Network is thriving, because cooking is both entertaining and therapeutic. Think of your time in the kitchen as your time to slow down, recharge, and be creative. If I were to quit my "day job" at Joey's I would go home and cook, for the sheer pleasure of cooking.

Pronto Joey's

Touring Tuscany

What is this place called Italy? As a kid, I never really asked that question. Growing up in Utica, NY, I took for granted my family's delicious Italian meals, our over-the-top, food-filled holidays, and our celebration of seasonal treats like figs and dandelion greens. Those traditions were set in stone—and I was only half-Italian! Luckily, my Irish-English mother had adopted my father's native cuisine. After he died, she kept his Italian spirit alive by cooking the foods he loved.

Little did I know that Italian food was my destiny. But by the time I fully appreciated its genius, I was way too busy with Joey's to travel to Italy. Then, on the 25th anniversary of my restaurant, I decided to write this cookbook. Every Saturday morning (the only time Joey's kitchen is quiet), I worked with my cookbook team, measuring ingredients (completely alien to me) and finding words to describe my instinctive approach to cooking. Our Saturday morning conversations inevitably led to Italy, the inspiration for many of Joey's recipes. That's when we decided to visit Tuscany. It was a leap of faith, leaving my restaurant for 10 days. But I had a well-trained staff of veterans and a new cell phone, with Joey's number on international speed-dial.

As soon as we arrived in Tuscany—this was in November 2006—we found our way to the deli of an Italian supermarket. I was immediately in my element, using broken Italian (and finger pointing) to communicate with the eager experts behind the counter. With an armful of carefully wrapped antipasti—olives, marinated eggplant and peppers, salami, prosciutto, Pecorino Romano and other l treasures—we were off to the neighborhood enoteca, where local grapes are made into wine. As tourists, we opted for the bottled red. But the locals literally pumped their wine, like fuel, into vessels of all sorts, from gallon-size vintage Chianti bottles to large plastic jugs.

Armed with the makings of our first Tuscan meal—and aided by a priceless GPS device—we wound our way to the small village of Donini, southwest of Florence. Our destination was the elegant 16th century villa restored by former Syracusan Beth Piper, MD. The property now combines three luxury apartments with a working farm—85 acres of vineyards and olive groves, It was definitely a spiritual experience, standing on the terrace that first afternoon, raising our glasses of local wine and nibbling antipasti. As far as we could see, there were neat rows of golden grapevines and silvery olive trees—old friends which have stood side-by-side for centuries.

I won't bore you with all the details of our trip, although you can feast on the Tuscan photographs sprinkled throughout these pages. I will say that, after an unforgettable lunch in a small, family restaurant, I turned to my team and said, "This validates everything I do at Joey's. Not just the way we prepare the food, but the whole atmosphere, the sense of celebration and family. Without ever setting foot in Italy, I knew, by instinct, how it should feel."

As much as I felt at home in Italy, I saw dramatic contrasts in our cultures. Americans have plenty of money but little time to cook—they eat in order to work. The Italians work in order to eat. Their example should inspire us rediscover the joy of sharing meals and enjoying each other.

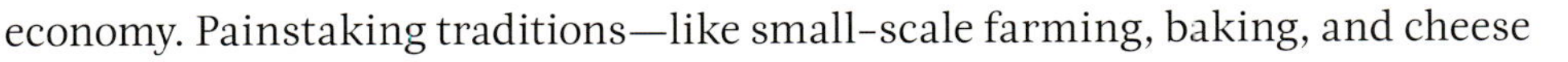

Not that life in Italy is euphoric. Like our own country, Italy is competing in a cutthroat global economy. Painstaking traditions—like small-scale farming, baking, and cheese making—are endangered. One of my new friends in Italy—Sandro, a fourth-generation baker in Donini—is one of the few who still bakes snow-white Tuscan bread, traditionally made without salt. He is known as the "couture" baker to Milan designers such as Armani and Gucci. But when Sandro retires in a few years, there will be no one to take over his family's bakery. More lucrative professions—in big cities—are luring Italy's younger generation, including its women.

Under the surface of Tuscany's great beauty, we saw some alarming trends. But, on my flight back home, I thought about my mother, who often worked two jobs while raising six children. For the love of Italian food, she made the time to cook and to gather us around the table. Her memory reassures me that the tradition of Italian cooking is pretty secure, over in Italy and here at home.

The Royal Treatment

Joey's routinely welcomes all types of celebrities—actors, entertainers, politicians, athletes and more. So it was no surprise when a representative of the Prince of Kuwait called one summer to inquire about booking the entire restaurant for the Prince and his entourage. That call led to daily, detailed phone conversations about the menu, security, and other aspects of what promised to be a grand evening. Soon everyone at Joey's was caught up in a whirlwind of preparation.

It was my job to handle the Prince's "people"—his publicist, security team, and diplomatic staff. Security was a huge issue: the day before the event, we had to close the restaurant so the security crew could comb through the dining room, kitchens, and parking lot. They even went up on the roof. Bomb-sniffing dogs checked out every inch of the facility. They didn't find any explosives, but they sure loved the smell of meatballs cooking.

Out of respect to the royal family, we were requested to make certain cultural accommodations. Our statue of Michelangelo's David and other classical works of art were either draped or removed for the evening. Finally, after weeks of all-consuming preparations and numerous menu revisions, the big night was upon us. The state police and Secret Service shut down the main intersection leading to Joey's. While a police helicopter hovered overhead, a procession of 10 limousines rolled into our parking lot.

My wife, Janice, stood at the entrance, ready to extend a royal welcome. Our eager staff lined the stairway leading to the dining room. I was still in the kitchen, nervously adding final touches to the lavish menu. Finally the Prince and his entourage stepped out of their limousines and silently filed into the restaurant. They were dressed in the traditional garb of flowing silk robes, with the men in turbans and the women in burkas.

As Janice warmly greeted our still-silent guests, she noticed that a pair of eyes, peeking out from a burka, looked strangely familiar—identical, in fact, to the eyes of a close friend. Then Janice realized that no one in the party had spoken a word, in Arabic or otherwise. Before she could relay her suspicions to me, I entered the dining room and approached the Prince's table, with the TV cameras rolling. But the Prince, with a haughty wave of his hand, dismissed me. I stopped in my tracks, feeling both embarrassed and furious.

That's when the Prince tore off his beard to reveal the face of my good friend and boating buddy, Skip Henning. Skip and a number of Joey's regulars had conspired all summer to pull this off! I had to admire the effort they poured into this elaborate, and very expensive, practical joke. What could I do but join in the celebration? It turned out to be a fantastic, memorable evening, with great food, good friends and many laughs.

Little did I know that the Prince of Kuwait scheme would come back to bite me one more time. A few weeks after the Prince's party, I received a call from the White House, as in 1600 Pennsylvania Avenue, Washington, D.C. On the line was a representative of then First Lady Hillary Clinton, who wanted to dine at Joey's during an upcoming visit to Syracuse. Let's just say that my reply was not according to White House protocol. "Yeah, right," I said. "You think I'm falling for this again? " And with that I slammed down the phone.

Joey's Wall of Fame

A few minutes later, New York State Assemblyman Michael Bragman called—simply stunned—to ask why I hung up on the First Lady. My face must have been beet red as I explained the elaborate ruse by the so-called Prince of Kuwait. With my tail between my legs, I called back the White House, apologized profusely, and invited the First Lady to be my guest at Joey's. She graciously accepted, came to the restaurant, ordered Chicken Française (see recipe, page 158), and loved it. Later, when she ran for the U.S. Senate, she asked Joey's to cater a local fund-raiser.

The moral of these stories? Whenever visiting dignitaries—celebrities, politicians and other VIPs—call Joey's, I take their reservations and promise to treat them just as we treat every other guest: like royalty.

Joey's at the TI Club

About a dozen years ago, Janice and I discovered the perfect antidote to the nonstop pace at Joey's: the tranquil, magical Thousand Islands region of the St. Lawrence River. Once a summer playground for America's wealthiest families, these islands are still sprinkled with historic, architectural jewels. One of those jewels—the Thousand Islands Club, a stone's throw from where we dock our boat on Wellesley Island—turned out to be more than we could resist.

Not that we didn't try. "Are you crazy?" I asked the club's owners (and our good friends) Mike and Julie Chavoustie, who first proposed the idea of a Joey's at the TI Club. "We need another restaurant like we need a hole in the head. We come up here to get away from the restaurant." But eventually we were seduced by the old-world charm of this 100-year-old landmark. Like the elaborate Boldt Castle, the TI Club was the brainchild of hotel magnate Charles C. Boldt. And like the castle, the TI Club was only partially constructed when Boldt died in 1916. Later completed by the partners who purchased Boldt's estate, the TI Club became a prominent polo and country club, beloved by locals, boaters and summer people alike.

With the Chavousties, Janice and I decided to restore the Club to its former luster. After a feverish round of remodeling, painting, scrubbing, and polishing, we opened Joey's at the TI Club in May 2005 for its first summer season. Like Joey's in Syracuse, the restaurant took off like fireworks. And as with the original Joey's, our success has been fuelled by family, especially my brothers Rick and Tony, my daughter, Aletea, and Janice's son Jared.

Key people from Joey's Syracuse staff and about 40 locals now complete the high-energy team that routinely serves about 350 diners on a Saturday night. We are proud to say that Joey's is the busiest restaurant in the Alexandria Bay area, as well as a popular and beautiful wedding destination. Running two restaurants—100 miles apart—doesn't leave much time to enjoy our cottage or boat. It certainly proves that I have a hole in my head. But it's truly a pleasure and an honor to play a role in the grand history of the Thousand Islands.

Appetizers

Antipasto

When it comes to reinventing everyday foods, the Italians are magicians. Their rustic techniques—such as sun-drying curing, pickling and aging—transform everyday staples into extraordinary delicacies. At Joey's, our antipasto platter simply celebrates these traditional delicacies. There is no formal recipe. These are simply suggestions: Use your own sense of taste and style to create a colorful array of contrasting flavors and textures. Allow enough of each item for each guest to try everything.

Lettuce, chopped
Italian cheeses, sliced, such as fresh mozzarella, provolone, Asiago, or Parmigiano-Reggiano

Salami, sliced

Prosciutto, sliced

Tuna or sardines, canned, packed in water, drained

Roasted Red Peppers (page 29)

Artichoke hearts, marinated, drained

Hard-boiled eggs, sliced

Hot cherry peppers or pepperoncini, pickled, drained

Kalamata olives

Vinaigrette, balsamic vinaigrette, or Caesar dressing

Cover a large serving tray with a bed of lettuce. Drizzle with salad dressing of choice. Arrange remaining ingredients to create an attractive display of contrasting colors, shapes, and textures.

Roasted Garlic

Roasting gives you the pure, sweet flavor of garlic without the bite. Roasted garlic is delicious spread warm on toasted bread and served with an assortment of olives.

Serves 4 to 6

4	**whole heads garlic**
2 tablespoons	**olive oil**

Preheat oven to 400 degrees F.

Cut off and discard the top third of garlic heads. Arrange whole garlic in an 8 x 8-inch ovenproof dish and drizzle with oil. Cover with foil. Bake for 20 to 30 minutes until the garlic releases its aroma. Remove from oven and cool. The soft, cooled cloves will pop out of their skins with a gentle squeeze. To store, cover whole cloves with olive oil in an airtight container.

Roasted Red Peppers

My pantry doesn't feel stocked unless I have roasted red peppers stored in olive oil. They make a great appetizer, either solo or paired with fresh mozzarella. They also add color, texture, and flavor to other dishes. I prefer to use only red bell peppers—as they ripen, they develop an incomparable sweetness.

Makes 4 cups

5	**fresh red bell peppers**
1 cup	**extra virgin olive oil**
3	**cloves garlic, minced**
5	**fresh basil leaves, chopped**
	Salt and black pepper, to taste

Preheat broiler. If you don't have a broiler, roast the peppers over a stovetop burner, using tongs to handle the peppers.

Place peppers on baking sheet and broil until skins blacken. Turn peppers so that each side is thoroughly charred. Transfer charred peppers to a paper bag, seal the bag, and set aside for about 15 minutes. When the peppers have cooled, use your fingertips to peel away the charred skin. Do not run the peppers under water—you'll wash away the flavor as well as the charred skin.

When the peppers are peeled, remove the stems. Open peppers, remove seeds, and slice away the inner ribs. Lay peppers flat and slice lengthwise in 1/2 to 1-inch wide strips, or larger if you prefer.

In a bowl, combine the oil, garlic, basil, and salt and pepper to taste. Place the pepper strips in a clean glass jar or resealable plastic container, add the oil mixture, and seal. To store, add enough oil to completely cover. Store in the refrigerator for up to 10 days. Bring to room temperature before serving as part of an antipasto platter—or simply with crusty bread and your favorite Italian cheese.

Shrimp Casino

This is just my interpretation of Clams Casino, a popular appetizer invented right here in the Empire State. I love the way the smoky bacon plays off the sweet shrimp in this dish.

Serves 4

12	large shrimp (U12)
½ cup	Joey's Seasoned Bread Crumbs (page 201)
2 tablespoons	grated Romano cheese
1 tablespoon	Olive Oil Blend (page 198)
¾ cup (6 ounces)	chopped bacon
3 tablespoons	butter
1	red bell pepper, diced
1	green bell pepper, diced
½	red onion, diced
1 ½ cups (10 ounces)	chopped spinach
	Juice of 1 lemon
1 tablespoon	extra dry vermouth
4 tablespoons	butter, cold, cut into 12 cubes
¼ cup	grated Asiago cheese
	Dash of paprika

Preheat oven to 400 degrees F.

Peel, devein, and butterfly the shrimp.

Arrange, cut-side up, in a single layer in ovenproof baking dish.

In a mixing bowl, combine bread crumbs with Romano cheese. In large saucepan, heat oil over medium-high heat. Add bacon and sauté until browned but not crisp. Add red and green peppers, onion, and spinach and sauté until softened, 3 to 4 minutes. Add butter to pan. Add bread crumb mixture and combine to form a paste.

Place 2 tablespoons of the mixture on top of each shrimp and press lightly. Squeeze lemon juice over shrimp and sprinkle with the vermouth. Dot with the butter cubes and sprinkle with the Asiago and a dash of paprika.

Bake for 20 minutes. Remove and serve immediately.

Escargot Joey

Babbalucci is the Italian word for snails. It didn't take a genius to figure out that the French word escargot would look more elegant on our menu. Names aside, it's flavor that counts, and this hors d'oeuvre tastes terrific.

Serves 4

1 tablespoon	**Olive Oil Blend (page 198)**
6	**cloves garlic, thinly sliced or finely chopped**
¼ cup	**coarsely chopped shallots**
2	**medium portobello mushrooms sliced into ¼-inch-thick slices**
2 cups	**fresh baby spinach**
2 tablespoons	**minced fresh flat leaf parsley**
24	**extra large escargot, we use canned and precooked**
8 tablespoons	**butter, cut into 8 pieces**
	Juice of ½ lemon
2 dashes	**Worcestershire sauce**
½ cup	**dry white wine, or Chicken Stock (page 54)**
½ cup	**grated Asiago cheese**
	Dash of paprika

Thoroughly rinse escargot in cold water, then drain and set aside.

Preheat oven to 450 degrees F.

Coat the bottom of a large sauté pan with oil and heat to medium high. Sauté garlic, shallots, and mushrooms for 2 minutes, to soften. Add spinach, parsley, escargot, butter, lemon juice, and Worcestershire sauce.

Swirl pan by the handle to combine ingredients and melt the butter. Add wine, bring to a bubble (almost but not quite a boil), and continue to cook to burn off the alcohol. Divide escargot mixture among four single-serving ramekins or pour into one 8 x 8-inch casserole. Sprinkle with Asiago and paprika.

Bake for 8 to 10 minutes until cheese melts. Remove from oven, and serve immediately.

Spinach Bread

This special bread is kind of like me: crusty on the outside, soft on the inside—and pretty colorful too.

Serves 4 to 6

½ loaf	**crusty Italian bread**
½ cup	**olive oil**
¼ pound	**bacon, diced**
3	**cloves garlic, peeled and minced**
2 ounces	**prosciutto, julienned**
12 ounces	**fresh spinach**
½ cup	**grated Romano cheese**
½ cup	**shredded mozzarella**
½ cup	**grated Asiago cheese**
8 to 12	**slices Roasted Red Peppers (page 29)**

Preheat oven to 375 degrees F.

Cut bread in half lengthwise and place, cut side up, on a baking sheet. Brush top of bread generously with 1/4 cup of the olive oil.

In a sauté pan over medium-high heat, cook the bacon until it just starts to turn crisp. Add garlic and remaining 1/4 cup olive oil and continue to sauté until garlic softens but does not brown.

Add prosciutto and spinach and continue to cook until spinach has wilted. Drain off excess liquid. Add Romano, combine thoroughly, and remove from heat.

Spread the mixture over bread. Sprinkle with the mozzarella and Asiago. Arrange the red pepper strips evenly across top of bread.

Bake for 7 to 8 minutes, or until the cheese starts to bubble and turn golden brown. Remove from oven and slice the bread so there is one slice of red pepper per portion. Transfer to a platter and serve immediately.

Arugula Crostini

This inspired combination—of peppery arugula and garlicky pesto—explodes on the tongue. I wish I could take the credit, but this creation comes courtesy of my wife, Janice.

Serves 4

½	loaf French baguette (2 inches in diameter), sliced in rounds ½-inch thick
¼ cup	Pesto Sauce (page 89)
1	bunch arugula
¼ cup	extra virgin olive oil
2 tablespoons	red wine vinegar
	Salt and pepper, to taste
2 ounces	prosciutto, sliced thin, cut into 1-inch squares
2 ounces	Parmigiano-Reggiano, shaved thin

Preheat oven to 350 degrees F.

Arrange baguette rounds on a baking sheet and toast in the oven until lightly browned. Remove from the oven and set aside to cool. When cool, spread a scant teaspoon of pesto on each toasted round.

Wash and dry the arugula, then tear into 1-inch pieces. In a medium bowl, whisk together oil and vinegar. Add salt and pepper to taste. Add arugula and toss. Top each toast round with a small mound of arugula mixture. Garnish with prosciutto and top with Parmigiano-Reggiano. Serve immediately.

Stuffed Mushrooms

When my grandparents came over from Italy, they must have been amazed by the abundance and excellence of meat in America. These stuffed mushrooms blend the flavors of the Old World with the riches of the new.

Makes 16 mushrooms

½ pound	**ground meatball mix (equal parts beef, pork, veal)**
½ pound	**Italian sausage, hot or sweet, removed from casing**
1	**egg**
¼ cup	**minced fresh parsley**
¼ cup	**minced shallots**
½	**red or green bell pepper, finely chopped**
¼ cup	**Joey's Seasoned Bread Crumbs (page 201)**
¼ cup	**grated Asiago cheese**
2 teaspoons	**granulated garlic (page 199)**
1 teaspoon	**salt**
1 teaspoon	**black pepper**
16	**large white mushrooms, at least 2 inches in diameter, preferably 3 to 4 inches in diameter**
¾ cup	**Joey's Marinara Sauce (page 86)**
¾ cup	**Chicken Stock (page 54)**
	Additional Asiago cheese, if desired

Preheat oven to 325 degrees F.

In a large bowl, combine the meatball mix and sausage. Add the egg, parsley, shallots, bell peppers, bread crumbs, Asiago, granulated garlic, salt, and pepper. Combine all ingredients—the easiest method is with your hands.

Clean mushrooms and remove the stems. In a large metal or ceramic baking dish, arrange mushroom caps, stem-side up, in a single layer. Fill each cap with a heaping tablespoon of stuffing. Top should be rounded but not tightly packed.

Combine marinara Sauce and chicken stock and carefully pour 1 cup of mixture over the stuffed mushrooms. Pour remaining sauce into the pan around the mushrooms. Tightly cover pan with aluminum foil and bake for 30 minutes. Remove foil and sprinkle with additional Asiago and return to oven to melt.

Before serving, baste mushrooms with sauce from bottom of pan. Serve as an appetizer or present on a platter, family style.

Grilled Romaine-Wrapped Mozzarella

Joey's is famous for its generous servings, but at heart I must be a thrifty Italian: I created this popular appetizer because I couldn't bear to toss those perfectly good romaine leaves that were too large for Caesar salad. This recipe calls for cooking the wraps on a grill, but you can also use a stove-top grill pan with ridges.

Serves 4

8 cups	**salted water**
8	**large romaine lettuce leaves**
8	**thin slices prosciutto**
½ pound	**fresh mozzarella, sliced ¼-inch thick**
	Black pepper, to taste
¼ cup	**olive oil**
2 tablespoons	**balsamic vinegar**
2 tablespoons	**chopped sun-dried tomatoes**
1 teaspoon	**granulated garlic (page 199)**

Prepare grill to medium-high (375 degrees F).

In a large stockpot, bring 8 cups water to a boil and add a pinch of salt. Prepare a bowl of ice water. Add the romaine leaves to the boiling water and blanche for 30 seconds. Transfer to bowl of ice water to stop cooking. Drain and pat dry. Spread romaine leaves on a clean, dry work surface. From the stem-side, cut a v-shaped notch in the lower center of each romaine leaf, for easier rolling. At the center of each leaf, layer 1 slice of prosciutto and 1 slice of mozzarella. Season with pepper. Roll and secure with a toothpick. Brush outside of wraps with the oil and grill over medium-high heat for 5 minutes, turning halfway through.

Meanwhile, in a small bowl, whisk together oil, vinegar, sun-dried tomatoes, and granulated garlic. Season with salt and pepper to taste. Remove wraps from the grill, slice each in half on the diagonal, and place four halves on each plate. Drizzle with dressing and serve immediately.

Fried Mozzarella

Don't confuse this delectable appetizer with the fried mozzarella sticks served in chain restaurants. Be sure to use fresh mozzarella, packed in its own liquid, preferably Mozzarella di Bufala from Italy.

Serves 4

	Olive Oil Blend (page 198) for frying
1 pound	**fresh mozzarella**
¼ cup	**flour**
2	**eggs, beaten**
1 cup	**Seasoned Bread Crumbs (page 201)**
2 tablespoons	**grated Asiago or Romano cheese**
1 cup	**Joey's Marinara Sauce (page 86)**

Add 1/2 inch oil to deep-sided frying pan and heat to 375 degrees F.

If using fresh mozzarella packed in water, pat dry (if it is still wet it will spatter and break through the batter when frying.) Slice the mozzarella into uniform 1/2-inch thick pieces. Dip the slices into the flour, then the egg, then the bread crumbs. With your fingers, lightly press bread crumbs into cheese to coat completely. When oil reaches 375 degrees F, add mozzarella and fry until golden brown, turning once, for a total of 4 to 5 minutes.

Meanwhile, heat the marinara sauce.

Remove mozzarella and drain on paper towels. To serve, pour warm marinara sauce over a serving plate or platter, then top with fried mozzarella, garnished with parsley and Asiago or Romano.

Fried Calamari

When I first served these crisp-tender calamari rings 30 years ago, I nicknamed them "Sicilian popcorn," because they sold so fast. They've anchored our appetizer menu since the day Joey's opened.

Serves 6

2 ½ pounds	**frozen calamari tubes and tentacles, thawed (typically, frozen calamari is available in 2 ½-pound packages)**
1 ¼ cups (10 ounces)	**fish fry breading (such as Golden Dipt)**
1 tablespoon	**granulated garlic**
1 tablespoon	**salt**
1 teaspoon	**black pepper**
2 cups	**peanut or canola oil, for deep frying**
1	**lemon, cut into wedges**
½ cup	**Marinara Sauce (page 86)**

Fill a deep fryer with oil (or pour 3 inches of oil into deep frying pan). Preheat oil to 375 degrees F.

While the oil is heating, rinse the thawed calamari and lightly pat dry with paper towels. Since there is no egg in the coating, the calamari needs to be damp so the breading will stick. In a shallow dish, combine the breading with the granulated garlic, salt, and pepper. Dredge the calamari pieces in the breading. Shake off excess.

When the oil is heated, drop the calamari into the deep fryer. Fry for 45 seconds to 1 minute, but no longer—calamari gets very tough very fast if overcooked. Remove calamari and drain on paper towels. Season with salt and pepper. Serve with fresh lemon wedges and marinara sauce for dipping.

Tips from Joey

If you don't have a deep-fryer, or a deep-fry thermometer, the oil is ready when you toss in a bread cube and it slowly sizzles, Also, I recommend using peanut or canola oil for frying, because they have a higher burn temperature than other oils.

I've cooked a lot of frozen calamari, and I have a strong preference for domestic brands. They tend to have better flavor and texture, and they are more tender when cooked. Thaw frozen calamari the day before you use it, by setting it in a bucket under cold running water until the calamari is thawed. Refrigerate until needed. Don't try to thaw it in a microwave. Trust me, just don't do it!

Calamari Salad

At Joey's, calamari is so popular that I once had an employee who did nothing but clean calamari and make ravioli. Today, we buy excellent calamari, frozen and already cleaned. (But we still make our ravioli from scratch!)

Serves 6

2 ½ pounds	frozen calamari, body and tentacles, thawed (frozen calamari is typically available in 2 ½-pound packages)
¼	lemon
3	stalks celery, sliced
1 cup	diced red bell pepper
½	red onion, diced
½ cup	large capers
12 to 15	Kalamata olives, pitted and halved
12 to 15	Spanish pimento-stuffed olives
8	pepperoncini, stemmed and sliced into rings
1 cup	chopped fresh basil
½ cup	olive oil
½ cup	white balsamic vinegar, or other white vinegar
1 ½ teaspoons	garlic powder
1 teaspoon	salt
1 ½ teaspoons	ground black pepper

Chop calamari bodies into ½-inch pieces, but do not cut tentacles. In a large stockpot, bring 8 cups of water to boil. Add salt and lemon. Add calamari. Boil for 1 hour, uncovered. Drain but do not rinse.

Transfer calamari to a bowl and toss to combine with remaining dressing ingredients. Cover tightly with plastic wrap and marinate overnight in the refrigerator.

To serve, line a shallow bowl or individual plates with chopped lettuce and spoon calamari and marinade over the lettuce.

A Tip from Joey

It's really worth finding white balsamic vinegar for this dish. While you can substitute another white vinegar, don't use red vinegar, or you'll end up with an eerily colored, pink-purple salad!

Calamari Steak

I first tasted this cutlet-style calamari 20 years in Mexico. Afterwards, I couldn't get it out of my head, so I tracked down a supplier in California, and I've been sharing this discovery with my calamari-crazed customers ever since.

Serves 4

1 pound	**calamari steaks**
1	**egg**
⅓ cup	**milk**
½ cup	**Seasoned Bread Crumbs (page 201)**
½ cup	**Olive Oil Blend (page 198)**
2 tablespoons	**butter, melted**
2 tablespoons	**olive oil**
	Juice of 1 lemon
⅓ cup	**grated Asiago cheese**

Preheat oven to 500 degrees F.

Cover the calamari steaks with plastic wrap and tenderize by pounding with a mallet, being careful not to tear the steaks. Combine the egg and milk in a shallow bowl. Dip calamari in the egg mixture, then coat with the bread crumbs, pressing with the palm of your hand to help adhere.

In large skillet, heat the oil to 350 degrees F. Add the calamari steaks one at a time and fry until nicely browned on both sides. Remove from pan and place in a shallow, ovenproof dish. Drizzle with the melted butter, olive oil, and lemon juice. Sprinkle with the cheese. Bake for 3 to 4 minutes, until cheese melts. Remove from the oven and slice into ¾-inch strips. Transfer to a serving plate and drizzle with pan juices.

A Tip from Joey

Calamari steaks, which may be labelled calamari cutlets, are available from your fishmonger or supermarket. They are cut from large calamari tubes and run through a "needling" machine to be flattened and tenderized.

Grilled Octopus Salad

I went crazy for this salad at a restaurant in Toronto. When I asked what made the octopus so tender, I could have sworn that the chef—who had very a heavy French accent—said they ran the octopus through the washing machine. I tried it at home, just once. Trust me, you'll be just as satisfied with the more conventional preparation below. You can special order octopus from your local fish market.

Serves 6

1	whole octopus (4 to 6 pounds), fresh or frozen
6 quarts	cold water
1 cup	red wine vinegar
1	lemon, halved
½ cup	crab boil, such as Old Bay Seasoning
1 teaspoon	salt
Marinade	
1 cup	olive oil
½	teaspoon salt
½ teaspoon	black pepper
1 teaspoon	granulated garlic
Salad	
½	fresh red bell pepper, diced
½	red onion, diced
½ cup	large Italian capers
Dressing	
⅓ cup	Olive Oil Blend (page 198)
¼ cup	balsamic vinegar
1 tablespoon	granulated garlic
1 tablespoon	minced fresh parsley or basil
	Salt and black pepper, to taste

If using frozen octopus, thaw 3 to 4 hours in a bucket of cold water. Replenish as needed with fresh, cold water.

In large stockpot, combine the octopus, water, vinegar, lemon halves, crab boil, and salt. Bring to a boil, then reduce heat to low, cover, and simmer for 3 hours, adding 8 more cups of water after the first hour. Drain the octopus, rinse under cold running water, and allow to cool enough to handle.

Use a small, very sharp knife (such as a boning or filet knife), to remove the head. Cut away all loose skin and discard the claw piece. You will be left with the body and the legs (tentacles).

Combine the marinade ingredients in a large bowl, add octopus, cover tightly with plastic wrap, and marinate 2 hours, or overnight, in the refrigerator. When ready to cook, preheat grill to high. Grill octopus for 5 minutes, turning frequently, to impart a charred flavor and make grill marks. Spread octopus on a large, cutting board and chop into bite-size pieces. In a large bowl, combine the red pepper, onion, and capers. Add the grilled octopus. Season with salt and ground pepper to taste. Add the olive oil, vinegar, granulated garlic, and parsley or basil. Just before serving, toss to combine. I like to serve this salad warm, but it is also very tasty chilled.

Clams Provençal

This simple dish is more French than Italian, but both cuisines share common ground, especially when it comes to celebrating Mediterranean seafood. Feel free to substitute mussels for the clams if they are available—they'll be just as delicious.

Serves 4 to 6

48	**littleneck clams (or mussels, scrubbed clean, beards removed)**
¼ cup	**olive oil**
1 cup	**minced fresh parsley or basil**
8	**cloves garlic, sliced**
4 tablespoons	**thinly sliced shallots**
1 ½ cups	**butter**
1 ½ cups	**dry white wine**

Soak clams or mussels in cold water and rinse three times to remove any sand. In a large saucepan, combine all the ingredients except the wine. Cover and place over medium-high heat. When garlic and shallots start to sizzle, remove cover, and add the wine.

Replace cover and continue to cook, shaking pan, until clams open—about 3 to 4 minutes. Serve in individual bowls, with the cooking liquid and your favorite Italian bread.

A Tip from Joey

When I cook this dish—or almost any dish—I shake the pan by the handle. The more you move these clams around, the faster they open. So shake that pan.

Shrimp Scampi

They tell me that scampi is the Italian word for prawn, or shrimp. On an Italian-American menu, we all know that scampi is shorthand for "good and garlicky." FYI, U-12 is restaurant lingo for "under 12" —it means you can expect about 12 shrimp per pound.*

Serves 4

12	large or jumbo shrimp (U-12)*
1 tablespoon	Olive Oil Blend (page 198)
2	anchovies
4 to 6	cloves garlic, peeled and minced
½ tablespoon	minced shallots
⅓ cup	dry white wine, or vermouth
8 tablespoons	butter, softened
1 tablespoon	flour
4 dashes	Worcestershire sauce
¼ cup	minced fresh parsley
	Dash of paprika

Peel and devein the shrimp.

In a large saute pan, heat the oil over medium–high heat. Add the shrimp and sear on both sides. Add the anchovies, garlic, and shallots. Cook until soft, 3 to 4 minutes. Add the wine and Worcestershire.

In a small bowl, blend the butter and flour, then add to the pan. Cook down to reduce and achieve a creamy consistency.

Transfer shrimp to a serving dish and top with sauce. Garnish with fresh parsley and paprika.

Oysters Rockefeller

The glamorous dish known as Oysters Rockefeller was created in 1899 by Jules Alciatore at Antoine's restaurant in New Orleans. To this day, his recipe remains top secret. For years, I tweaked and tested every ingredient, in pursuit of the original perfection. In the process, I created a version I like even better. I recommend using Long Island Blue Points if you can get them.

Serves 4, 3 oysters per serving

12	**fresh oysters, shucked, left on the half shells**
1 tablespoon	**Olive Oil Blend (page 198)**
½	**onion, minced**
4 tablespoons	**butter**
1 tablespoon	**minced garlic**
1 cup	**diced pancetta**
2 ounces	**anisette**
2 cups	**chopped fresh spinach**
6 tablespoons	**grated Romano cheese,**
1 cup	**Bechamel Sauce (page 201)**
¼ cup	**grated Asiago cheese**
	Juice of 1 lemon

Preheat oven to 450 degrees F.

In large frying pan, heat the oil over medium heat. Add the onion and pancetta and cook until lightly browned. Add the butter and melt. Add the garlic and cook until fragrant. Remove from heat and transfer pancetta mixture to a mixing bowl.

Add anisette to the frying pan and warm over medium heat, but do not boil. When anisette is warm, flambé by lighting with long-tipped match or lighter. As soon as flame subsides, immediately add spinach. When spinach is wilted, drain and add to pancetta mixture. Add Romano and combine thoroughly.

Use crumpled aluminum foil to create a bed in a large baking dish—this will prevent the oysters from tipping. Arrange the oysters on the foil. Divide spinach mixture equally over oysters. Ladle a little bechamel sauce over each oyster. Sprinkle with the Asiago. Bake for about 10 minutes, until the cheese starts to melt and turn golden brown. Remove from the oven and pour the pan juices over the oysters.

Transfer the oysters in their half shells to a serving plate. Drizzle sparingly with lemon juice and serve immediately.

Soups

Salads

Sides

Chicken Stock

Growing up, we always had something simmering on the stove: sauce, soup, or stock. I'm a big advocate of homemade chicken stock, because I think it adds incomparable flavor. It's also very energy-efficient. Ten minutes of prep time (and a few undemanding hours on the stove) will yield at least 3 quarts of beautiful stock.

Makes 3 quarts

1	large (5-pound) roasting chicken
3	bay leaves
5	cloves garlic, smashed
1 tablespoon	black peppercorns
2	onions, chopped
2	carrots, chopped
3	stalks celery, chopped
½	bunch parsley, chopped
4 quarts	cold water

In a 16-quart stockpot, combine all the ingredients and add enough cold water to cover. The cold water will help ensure a nice, clear stock. Place the stockpot over medium-high heat, bring to a boil, reduce heat to low, and simmer, uncovered, for 3 hours. Do not stir, but add cold water, as needed, to keep the chicken and vegetables covered.

After 3 hours, remove stockpot from stove, strain the stock and discard vegetables.* Allow stock to cool, then skim fat from top. Remove skin and bones from chicken and reserve meat for another use.

Chicken stock will keep—tightly sealed—for 1 week in the refrigerator or 3 months in the freezer.

Tips from Joey

Stock versus Broth: A broth is a soup base made with only the carcass or bones. A stock includes meat. They can be used interchangeably in soup recipes. Soup made with broth will be clearer and lighter than the same soup made with a stock. They will be just as delicious!

After straining the vegetables from the stock, puree them with a little bit of stock—it makes a nice addition to other soups or stews as a thickener or flavor enhancer.

Veal Stock

Makes 2 quarts

Follow the recipe for Chicken Stock (above), but replace the roasting chicken with 3 pounds split veal knucklebones (preferred) or other veal bones as available.

Beef Stock

Homemade beef stock is like homemade chicken stock—nothing compares to the real thing. It's a bit more work but absolutely worth the effort.

Makes 2 quarts

3 pounds	**beef shanks, cut into 2-inch chunks, or split oxtails, or both**
2	**onions, quartered**
2	**carrots, chopped**
2	**celery stalks, chopped**
5	**cloves garlic, smashed**
About 14 cups	**cold water**
½	**bunch parsley, chopped**

Preheat oven to 425 degrees F.

Lightly oil a large roasting pan, add the beef, and roast for 15 minutes. Add the remaining ingredients and roast, stirring occasionally to keep vegetables from burning, about 40 minutes. Transfer the meat and vegetables to a 16-quart stockpot. Deglaze the roasting pan and add the cooking juices and browned bits to the stockpot.

Add 14 cups of cold water to stockpot (or enough to cover the meat and vegetables). Bring to a boil over medium heat and skim off any fat or impurities that rise to the surface. Reduce heat to low and simmer for about 30 minutes. Skim again, then add parsley. Continue to simmer, uncovered, for about 4 hours, skimming fat as needed. Strain the stock, allow to cool, and store in the refrigerator. Skim fat before using.

Tips from Joey

If you don't have time to make your own stock, there are some really good soup bases available. I recommend that you read the ingredients on the label and look for soup bases that do not have a lot of salt. I like my soup base to be full of flavor, not just salt. Try different brands until you find the one you like best. Don't use bouillon cubes as a substitute—they are almost pure salt and have very little flavor!

To deglaze a roasting pan or skillet: Pour off all the fat or oil from the pan. While the pan is still hot, add about 1/4 cup of liquid; water, or better yet, use something that will add more flavor to your stock—some stock or broth, wine, beer, or other spirits. With a large wooden spoon, scrape up all the browned bits of meats and vegetables that are stuck to the bottom. Add to the stock pot.

Bean Soup Base

I use this thick, fragrant base as a foundation for my hearty bean soups, like Greens and Beans (below).

Makes about 3 quarts

6 ounces	salt pork
¼ cup	Olive Oil Blend (page 198)
1 pound	pancetta or high-quality bacon, diced
2 tablespoons	smoked ham soup base, optional
1	onion, diced
6	cloves garlic, minced
7 (15.5 ounce)	cans cannellini beans, undrained
4 cups	Chicken Stock (page 54)
2 teaspoons	ground black pepper

In a 12-quart stockpot, heat the oil over medium-high heat. Add the salt pork and sauté until lightly browned. Add the pancetta or bacon and cook until brown not crisp. Add the onion and optional smoked ham base and lightly brown. Add the garlic and lightly brown. Add the undrained beans, chicken stock, and ground black pepper. Bring the mixture to a boil and remove from heat. Retrieve and discard the salt pork. Allow the bean base to cool, then transfer to 1-quart or 2-quart containers. Store, tightly sealed, for up to 5 days in the refrigerator or up to 3 months in the freezer

A Tip from Joey

Smoked ham base can be more difficult to find than most soup base products. If it's not available, don't worry. Your stock will be fine without it.

Greens and Beans

When customers tell me that my greens and beans are as good as their mothers', I am honored.

Serves 4 to 6

1 ½ quarts	Bean Soup Base (see above)
1	head escarole, washed, coarsely chopped

In a stockpot, bring 4 quarts of salted water to a boil. Add the escarole to boiling water and cook until tender, about 2 minutes. Immediately drain and plunge into a cold-water bath (4 cups cold water and 4 cups ice) to halt cooking. Thoroughly drain the escarole in a colander.

Add the bean base to the stockpot, stir in the escarole, and gently simmer over low heat for 10 minutes to heat through. If the mixture seems too thick, thin with additional chicken stock.

For a meatier version, add chopped cooked bacon, or sliced, cooked sausage when you add the escarole to the bean soup base.

Lobster Stock

For maximum flavor, I recommend using uncooked lobster shells, which you can buy at your fish market. Cooked lobster shells will not add much flavor.

Makes 1 ½ quarts

4-6	uncooked lobster shells
½ cup	tomato paste
3 cups	uncooked shrimp shells
2	onions, chopped
2	carrots, chopped
3	stalks celery, chopped
2 quarts	cold water
1	bay leaf
2 teaspoons	crushed black peppercorns
1	lemon, cut in half

Preheat oven to 350 degrees F.

Rub the lobster shells with a little tomato paste, arrange in a roasting pan, and roast for ½ hour. Do not roast the shrimp shells, which are too delicate to withstand the heat.

In a large stockpot, place the roasted lobster shells and the shrimp shells, plus the vegetables.

Add 2 quarts cold water, or enough to cover shells and vegetables, then add the bay leaf, crushed black peppercorns, and lemon halves. Bring to a boil, reduce heat, and simmer, partially covered, for 2 hours, skimming occasionally after the first hour. Add more water as needed to keep the shells covered. Strain and allow to cool before storing in refrigerator.

Shrimp, Scallop, and Leek Bisque

This recipe requires a little effort, but its velvety consistency and rich flavor will knock your socks off. The bisque comes together in three simple steps—searing the shellfish, making the roux, and preparing the lobster base.

Serves 4

2 tablespoons	**Olive Oil Blend (page 198)**
8	**medium to large shrimp, peeled and deveined**
8	**large scallops, rinsed and dried with paper towels**
4 tablespoons	**butter**
¼ cup	**flour**
1 tablespoon	**olive oil**
1	**leek, white stalk only, cleaned and chopped, or ½ cup finely chopped shallots**
2 cups	**Lobster Stock (page 58), heated**
1 tablespoon	**lobster soup base**
2 cups	**heavy cream**
¼ teaspoon	**seafood seasoning blend, such as Old Bay**
2 teaspoons	**snipped fresh chives**

In a large skillet, heat the blended oil over high heat until it begins to smoke. Add the shrimp and quickly sear but do not burn. When the shrimp are firm and lightly browned, remove from skillet and reserve. Follow same method to sear the scallops.

To make the roux, place a small saucepan over medium heat and melt the butter. Sift the flour through a sieve directly into the saucepan. Cook for several minutes, whisking constantly to blend. Set aside.

In a large saucepan, heat the olive oil to medium hot. Add the leek (or shallots) and gently sauté for 5 minutes, or until translucent but not browned. Meanwhile, in a separate saucepan, heat the lobster stock. Add the hot lobster stock to the leeks. Stir in the lobster base. Bring to a boil, reduce heat to low, and add the heavy cream. Add the seafood seasoning and stir to combine.

Thicken the bisque by slowly stirring in the reserved roux. Continue to simmer over low heat until bisque is heated through. To serve, place 2 scallops and 2 shrimp in each of 4 warmed bowls. Pour the bisque into the bowls and garnish with chives.

Pasta Fagioli

After a memorable meal in a beautiful Tuscan home, our host (a bread baker by day, opera singer by night) gave us each a package of dried Tuscan beans. His gesture spoke volumes about the Tuscan reverence for the humble bean—known in Italy as "the poor man's meat."

Serves 4 to 6

1 ½ quarts	**Bean Soup Base, (page 56)**
1 cup	**Joey's Marinara Sauce (page 86)**
½ cup	**ditalini, cooked al dente, drained and rinsed**
½	**bunch fresh Italian parsley, stemmed and finely chopped**
2 cups	**Chicken Stock (page 54)**
1 teaspoon	**crushed red pepper flakes**
¼ cup	**grated Parmigiano-Reggiano cheese**

In a large saucepan, combine the marinara sauce, bean soup base, parsley, and chicken stock. Heat over medium heat until warmed through.

Add the red pepper flakes and the ditalini just before serving (or it will dry out).

Garnish with freshly grated Parmigiano-Reggiano.

Minestrone

When I was a kid, we had minestrone for dinner at least once a week. We couldn't wait to dig in, because my mother always added 2 whole garlic cloves. If you found the first clove, you won a quarter. If you found the second, you won a dime. If you were clever enough to bring your own garlic and slip it into your soup, you were busted, every time. This recipe makes a lot of soup. You could cut the ingredients in half—or you could invite all your family and friends and talk about the old days!

Makes 8 quarts

¼ cup	**Olive Oil Blend (page 198)**
8 ounces	**salt pork, cut into in large chunks**
2	**cloves garlic, minced**
1	**large onion, diced**
2	**stalks celery, diced**
5 quarts	**Beef Stock (page 55) or Veal Stock (page 54)**
1 cup (8 ounces)	**dried split peas**
1 cup (8 ounces)	**dried lentils**
3	**carrots, cut bite-size**
1 (28-ounce)	**can tomatoes, crushed in thick purée**
2 (15-ounce)	**cans cannellini beans, drained**
1 (15-ounce)	**can garbanzo beans, drained**
1 (15-ounce)	**can red kidney beans, drained**
1	**medium zucchini, diced**
1	**medium yellow squash, diced**
½ pound	**fresh green beans, cut into ½-inch pieces**
1 pound	**ditalini, cooked al dente, drained and rinsed**
½	**head escarole, chopped**
	Salt and pepper, to taste
½ cup	**grated Parmigiano-Reggiano cheese**

In a 16-quart stockpot, heat the oil to medium hot. Add the salt pork and sauté until lightly browned. Add the garlic, onion, and celery and sauté until softened. Add the beef stock and bring to a boil. Add the split peas and lentils and return to a boil. Reduce heat to low and simmer for 30 minutes, adding cold water as needed.

Skim off any fat that rises to top. Add the carrots and tomatoes in purée. Continue to simmer for 30 minutes or until carrots are tender. Add the drained cannellini, garbanzo, and kidney beans, then the zucchini, yellow squash, and green beans.

Prepare the escarole: Bring a separate pot of salted water to a boil. Add the washed escarole and cook for 2 minutes. Drain and immediately plunge into a cold water bath (4 cups cold water, 4 cups ice) to stop cooking. Drain the escarole again and add to the minestrone Add the ditalini and stir to combine. Season with salt and pepper.

If you are like me and prefer a thicker minestrone: In a small bowl, thoroughly combine 1 tablespoon of cornstarch and 1 cup of cold water. Add to the soup, stir to combine and return to a simmer. Remove from heat. Let the minestrone sit for a few minutes to thicken. Serve with Parmigiano-Reggiano.

A Tip from Joey

I frequently choose my minestrone soup vegetables according to what is available for the season. About the only vegetable I don't recommend for minestrone is broccoli,or other vegetables that will break apart during long cooking times. Also, in my opinion, broccoli imparts a strong flavor that doesn't blend well with minestrone soup.

Butternut Squash with Roasted Garlic Soup

Squash was introduced to Italy in the 16th century, as a celebrated import from the New World. That makes this sunset-hued soup a truly Italian-American collaboration.

Serves 4 to 6

2	carrots, chopped
2	stalks celery, chopped
1	onion, chopped
4 pounds	butternut squash, peeled and cubed
4 cups	Chicken Stock (page 54)
1 tablespoon	chicken soup base (see page 200)
4	cloves Roasted Garlic (page 26)
1 cup	heavy cream
	Salt and black pepper, to taste
2 tablespoons	minced fresh parsley
	Dash of grated nutmeg

In a medium saucepan, place the carrots, celery, and onion. Cover with cold water, bring to a boil, reduce heat to medium, and cook until the carrots are soft. Drain and reserve.

Place the squash in a 12-quart stockpot, cover with cold water and bring to a boil. Reduce heat to medium and cook until the squash is easily pierced with a fork. Drain and plunge into a cold water bath (4 cups cold water, 4 cups ice) to stop cooking. Drain squash again.

In a food processor, purée the squash with the roasted garlic and previously cooked vegetables. Return the mixture to stockpot. Add the chicken stock (4 cups will make a thick soup; for a thinner consistency, add extra stock). Add the chicken base and stir to combine over medium-high heat. Bring to a boil, reduce to a simmer, and stir in the heavy cream. Season with salt and pepper. Stirring constantly, simmer until heated through. Pour into bowls and garnish with parsley or nutmeg.

Chicken Soup Pastina

The last-minute addition of the tiny pastina gives this soup its unique Italian character, but we can't take the credit for chicken soup, the universal symbol of comfort.

Makes about 2 quarts

2 tablespoons	**olive oil**
2	**carrots, diced**
3	**stalks celery, diced**
2 quarts	**Chicken Stock (page 54)**
2 tablespoons	**chicken soup base (see page 200)**
1 cup	**cooked, pulled chicken**
1 tablespoon	**cornstarch**
¼ cup	**cold water**
1 cup	**dried pastina, cooked al dente, drained and rinsed**
¼ cup	**minced Italian parsley**

In an 8-quart stockpot, heat the olive oil over medium-high heat. Add the onions, celery, and carrots. Gently sauté the vegetables to release their flavors, but do not brown. Add the chicken stock, then stir in the chicken base. Bring to a boil, reduce heat to low, and simmer, uncovered, for 1 hour. Add the chicken.

In a small bowl, thoroughly blend the cornstarch with cold water. Drizzle into soup and stir to combine. Add the pastina. Heat to warm. Before serving, garnish with the parsley.

Italian Wedding Soup

As the name suggests, this soup is a favorite first course at Italian-American weddings. But that's not how it earned its name: In Italian, it's called Minestrona Maritata, to salute the perfect marriage of escarole and meatballs! One can only hope the bride and groom are as well matched.

Serves 4 to 6

2 quarts	**Chicken Stock (page 54)**
1 tablespoon	**chicken soup base (see page 200)**
½	**head escarole, thoroughly washed and shredded**
16	**mini Joey's Meatballs (page 125), made a scant 1-inch in diameter**
1 cup	**acini di pepe, pastina, or orzo, cooked al dente, drained and rinsed**
½ cup	**grated Romano cheese**

In an 8-quart stockpot, combine the chicken stock and chicken base and bring to boil over medium-high heat. Add the meatballs, reduce heat to low, and simmer for about 8 minutes. Add the escarole and pasta and continue to simmer until heated through. Garnish with the Romano and serve.

Stracciatella Romano

Stracciatella means "little rags" in Italian. This simple soup is soothing, delicious, and delicate enough for the bambinos.

Serves 4 to 6

2 quarts	**Chicken Stock (page 54)**
1 tablespoon	**chicken soup base (see page 200)**
½ pound	**fresh spinach, chopped**
3	**eggs**
4 ounces	**pastina, cooked al dente, drained and rinsed (optional)**
¼ cup (2 ounces)	**grated Romano cheese**

In a 4-quart saucepan, bring the chicken stock and chicken base to boil over medium-high heat. Stir in the spinach.

In a small bowl, whisk together eggs. Drizzle the eggs into the soup and stir with a fork or a whisk to separate the eggs into little shreds. Continue to boil for about 1 minute, while continuing to stir.

If desired, add the pastini, reduce heat to medium, and heat through.

Before serving, garnish with the Romano.

Salad of Dandelion Greens

At Joey's, we make a big deal out of dandelion greens—in the Italian kitchen, they're a sure sign of spring. Lightly dressed, these bitter, delicate leaves make a beautiful palate cleanser. In the restaurant, we use commercially grown dandelion greens. But along the New York State Thruway, I've seen people picking wild dandelion greens. A word of warning to these fearless foragers: once the dandelions have flowered, the greens are just too tough to eat.

Serves 4

12 ounces	**fresh dandelion greens**
¼ cup	**olive oil**
2 tablespoons	**balsamic vinegar**
1 teaspoon	**dried basil**
1 teaspoon	**granulated garlic**
1 teaspoon	**salt**
½ cup	**chopped red onion**
½ cup	**canned, drained chickpeas**
	Curls of Parmigiano-Reggiano for garnish*

Remove and discard about 1 inch from the root end of the dandelion greens. Thoroughly wash the greens: fill the sink with cold water, add the greens, let them soak for several minutes, then swish them through the water. Remove the greens, drain the sink, and refill with cold water. Repeat the washing process twice more, to remove all dirt and sand. Drain the greens and dry well.

In a large salad bowl, whisk together the olive oil, vinegar, basil, granulated garlic, and salt. Add the dandelion greens, onion, and chickpeas and toss gently. Garnish with Parmigiano-Reggiano curls, made by the scraping against the cheese with a vegetable peeler.

Tomato and Cucumber Salad

Sweet, juicy tomatoes and crisp, cool cucumbers make a quick, refreshing salad.

Serves 4

¼ cup	extra virgin olive oil
2 tablespoons	balsamic vinegar
1 ½ teaspoons	granulated garlic
4	large, ripe tomatoes cut into bite-size wedges
2	medium cucumbers, peeled, sliced lengthwise, cut into 1-inch pieces
1	small red onion, chopped
6	fresh basil leaves, minced
	Salt and ground black pepper, to taste

In a large, stainless steel bowl, whisk together the olive oil, vinegar, and granulated garlic. Add the tomatoes, red onion, and cucumbers. Toss to combine. Season with salt and pepper. Serve immediately.

Joey's Caesar Salad

It's hard to find an American menu without Caesar salad, but an authentic Caesar salad, made tableside? Not so common! This version is a showstopper, if you pay attention to the details. Before you begin, be sure the bowl and the romaine leaves are thoroughly clean and dry. Also, be sure the egg yolk is completely separated from the egg white. And always add the lemon juice after the egg yolk.

Serves 4

1	**large head romaine, washed, dried, and torn or cut into 1-inch pieces**
2	**cloves garlic, mashed**
1 teaspoon	**anchovy paste, or 4 anchovies, mashed**
1 tablespoon	**Dijon mustard**
1 tablespoon	**Worcestershire sauce**
2	**egg yolks, carefully separated**
	Splash of balsamic vinegar
½ cup	**olive oil**
	Juice of 1 lemon
1 cup	**Croutons (see below)**
1 cup	**grated Romano cheese, plus additional cheese to pass**
	Ground black pepper, to taste

In a large wooden salad bowl, mash together the garlic and anchovies. Whisk in the Dijon mustard and Worcestershire sauce. Whisk in the egg yolks and vinegar. Continue to whisk while slowly drizzling the olive oil to create a thick emulsion. Add the romaine, then the lemon juice, croutons, and Romano. Toss to combine thoroughly. Allow your guests to garnish with black pepper and additional Romano, to taste.

Croutons, Italian Style

This is a thrifty and tasty way to recycle bread that's a few days old. I use Italian bread with a heavy crust for extra crunch, but a baguette works well too.

1	**loaf Italian or French bread (or whatever you have on hand)**
	Extra virgin olive oil
	Granulated garlic
	Salt and pepper, to taste
	Romano cheese, freshly grated
	Optional: dried Italian herbs: basil, thyme, oregano, to taste

Preheat oven to 375 degrees F.

Cut the bread into cubes about 1-inch square. Arrange the bread cubes on a cookie sheet and bake until toasted golden brown, about 10 to 15 minutes. Remove from oven and place bread cubes in a mixing bowl. While the bread is still hot, drizzle with olive oil. Sprinkle with grated romano cheese, granulated garlic salt, and pepper, and, if desired, dried herbs. Fresh made croutons are best used right away.

A Tip from Joey

Tossing a Caesar salad is not a task for the tentative or hurried chef. Toss vigorously for 3 minutes—trust me. The more you work the dressing through the romaine leaves, the better it will be.

Mozzarella and Tomato Salad with Basil

Vine-ripened tomatoes and fresh mozzarella look stunning side-by-side—and taste heavenly together. Fresh basil is the perfect accent for this classic pairing. To release the beautiful basil flavor, shred the leaves chiffonade-style: stack about 6 fresh basil leaves and roll them together lengthwise. Using a sharp knife, make thin crosswise cuts into the cylinders of basil—the spirals will unroll into fine shreds, releasing that incomparable basil aroma and flavor.

Serves 4

3	large, vine-ripened tomatoes
½ pound	fresh mozzarella—the freshest and best-quality available
12	fresh basil leaves
¼ cup	extra virgin olive oil
2 tablespoons	balsamic vinegar
1 ½ teaspoons	granulated garlic
	Salt and freshly ground black pepper, to taste

Halve the tomatoes, then cut into slices 1/4-inch thick. Slice the mozzarella into 1/2- inch-thick rounds. Chiffonade the basil leaves.

On a serving platter, alternate the tomato and mozzarella slices, overlapping slightly. Drizzle with the olive oil and balsamic vinegar, then sprinkle with the shredded basil. Season with granulated garlic, salt and pepper.

A Tip from Joey

Vine-ripened tomatoes are now widely available, year-round, so there's no reason to settle for pale, mealy, tasteless tomatoes. If your tomatoes aren't perfectly ripe when you get them home, let them sit out at room temperature for a few days to ripen naturally.

Rosemary Roasted Potatoes

Perfect with chicken, perfect with pork, perfect with beef or veal: these easy potatoes work well with almost anything.

Serves 4 to 6

8	medium red potatoes
¼ cup	olive oil
1 tablespoon	granulated garlic
	Salt and pepper to taste
2 tablespoons	dried rosemary, or 2 sprigs fresh rosemary

Preheat oven to 350 degrees F.

Wash and quarter the potatoes but do not peel. In a large saucepot, boil the potatoes in salted water for 15 minutes. Drain and arrange in a baking dish. Drizzle with the olive oil, sprinkle with granulated garlic, and season with salt and pepper. Sprinkle with rosemary. Roast the potatoes for 25 minutes giving them a stir halfway through.

Broccoli Rabe (Rapini)

Broccoli rabe, or rapini, is more delicate—and slightly more bitter—than regular broccoli. It serves as a great excuse to break out the garlic and hot pepper. When I visited Tuscany, this was the first dish I prepared on Italian soil.

Serves 6

2	bunches (1 pound each) broccoli rabe (rapini)
¾ cup	Olive Oil Blend (page 198)
4	cloves garlic, thinly sliced
	Salt and black pepper, to taste
	Crushed hot pepper flakes, to taste

In a large saucepan, bring 2 quarts of salted water to a boil. While water is heating, trim and discard stalks from the rapini. Add the florets and leaves to boiling water and cook 4 to 5 minutes, until al dente or crisp-tender. Drain the rapini (reserving 1/4 cup cooking water) and transfer to an ice bath (4 cups cold water, 4 cups ice) to stop cooking. Drain.

In a large skillet, heat the oil over medium-high heat. Add the garlic and sauté until edges are lightly browned. Add the rapini and heat through. Season with salt, pepper, and crushed red pepper flakes. For more tender rapini, add 1/4 cup reserved cooking water and continue to cook to desired texture. Serve immediately.

As an appetizer, serve this simple dish with Italian bread to soak up the garlicky oil. To make it a meal, add 1/2 cup chicken stock to the rapini mixture. Add 8 ounces cooked Italian sausage, sliced into bite–size pieces. Heat through and toss with 1 pound pasta, such as macaroni or orchiette, cooked and drained. Sprinkle with grated Romano cheese.

A Tip from Joey

Blanching may seem like a nuisance, but it makes a big difference. Blanching softens the vegetable's texture, makes it less bitter, and keeps it bright green.

Utica Greens

In Central New York, restaurants are often judged by the Utica greens they serve. This signature dish of my native city is a staple at Joey's—and a popular lunch with our regulars at the bar. I grew up on spicy Utica greens. Back in the day, I would often end an evening at one of Utica's late-night clubs with a diner breakfast of steak, eggs, and Utica greens.

Serves 6

2	**heads escarole (about 2 pounds)**
½ cup plus 2 tablespoons	**olive oil**
½ cup	**sliced onion**
½ cup (4 ounces)	**finely chopped pancetta—or half prosciutto and half cooked bacon**
5	**cloves garlic, thinly sliced**
3	**hot cherry peppers in vinegar, drained, stemmed, seeded, and chopped**
½ cup	**Chicken Stock (page 54)**
½ cup	**Seasoned Bread Crumbs (page 201)**
	Salt and black pepper, to taste
½ cup	**grated Asiago cheese**

Preheat oven to 400 degrees F.

Because escarole tends to be sandy, wash it thoroughly by filling the sink with cold water and swishing the leaves through the water. Drain the water from the sink and repeat the process twice more (or use prewashed escarole). Drain well and cut the escarole into 1-inch strips.

In a large pot, bring 6 quarts of salted water to a boil, add the escarole and blanche for 2 minutes. Drain the pot and plunge the escarole into an ice bath (4 cups cold water, 4 cups ice) to stop cooking. Drain thoroughly.

In a large skillet, heat 1/2 cup olive oil over medium heat. Add the onion and pancetta and cook for 5 minutes to soften. Do not brown. Increase heat to medium-high, and add the garlic. Sauté until lightly browned, then add the escarole, peppers, and chicken broth.

Combine thoroughly and cook until escarole is wilted. Season with salt and pepper.

Transfer the mixture to a 2-quart baking dish. In small bowl, combine the bread crumbs with 2 tablespoons of olive oil. Spread the moistened bread crumbs over the escarole, then sprinkle with Asiago. Bake until the cheese melts, about 15 minutes.

A Tip from Joey

Feel free to add your own signature touch to this dish, such as sliced, cooked Italian sausage or cubed Roasted Rosemary Potatoes (page 74).

Eggplant Parmigiana

Everyone's favorite eggplant dish, it's also a favorite of vegetarians and folks who are trying to eat less red meat. I prefer to use Romano instead of the traditional Parmigiano-Reggiano in this recipe, because its milder flavor doesn't overwhelm the eggplant.

Serves 9 to 12

3 pounds	**eggplant (about 4 medium)**
½ cup	**flour, for dusting**
4	**eggs**
2 cups	**milk**
3 cups	**Seasoned Bread Crumbs (page 201)**
3 cups	**oil (peanut, canola, or vegetable)**
2 cups	**Joey's Mother's Sunday Sauce (page 85)**
2 cups	**grated mozzarella**
1 cup	**grated Romano cheese**

Peel and slice each eggplant lengthwise into 1/4-inch slices. Lightly dust eggplant slices with flour, to prevent discoloration.

In a shallow bowl, whisk together the eggs and milk. Place breadcrumbs in a shallow pan, a pie plate works well. Dip eggplant slices in the egg mixture, then the breadcrumbs. Press crumbs into eggplant to help them adhere.

In a deep, 12-inch skillet, heat oil to 350 degrees F. Test by tossing in a few bread crumbs. Oil is ready when crumbs sizzle. Add eggplant slices and fry for 2 to 3 minutes on each side. Drain slices on paper towels and stack on edges, angled against each other.

Preheat oven to 350 degrees F.

To assemble, spread 1/2 cup Joey's Sunday sauce over the bottom of a 9 x 12-inch baking pan. Cover with a layer of eggplant slices, overlapping the edges slightly. With a spatula, lightly press eggplant slices into the sauce. Cover eggplant with 1/2 cup sauce, 1/3 cup Romano, and 1/2 cup mozzarella. Make another layer of eggplant slices, arranging in the opposite direction from first layer. Cover eggplant with another 1/2 cup sauce, 1/3 cup Romano, and 1/2 cup mozzarella. Make a third layer of eggplant slices, arranging in same direction as bottom layer. Cover with remaining sauce, remaining Romano and remaining mozzarella. Bake immediately (otherwise eggplant becomes soggy) for 40 minutes. Let cool for 15 minutes before slicing into 9 to 12 servings.

JOEY'S
CLASSIC
ITALIAN DINING

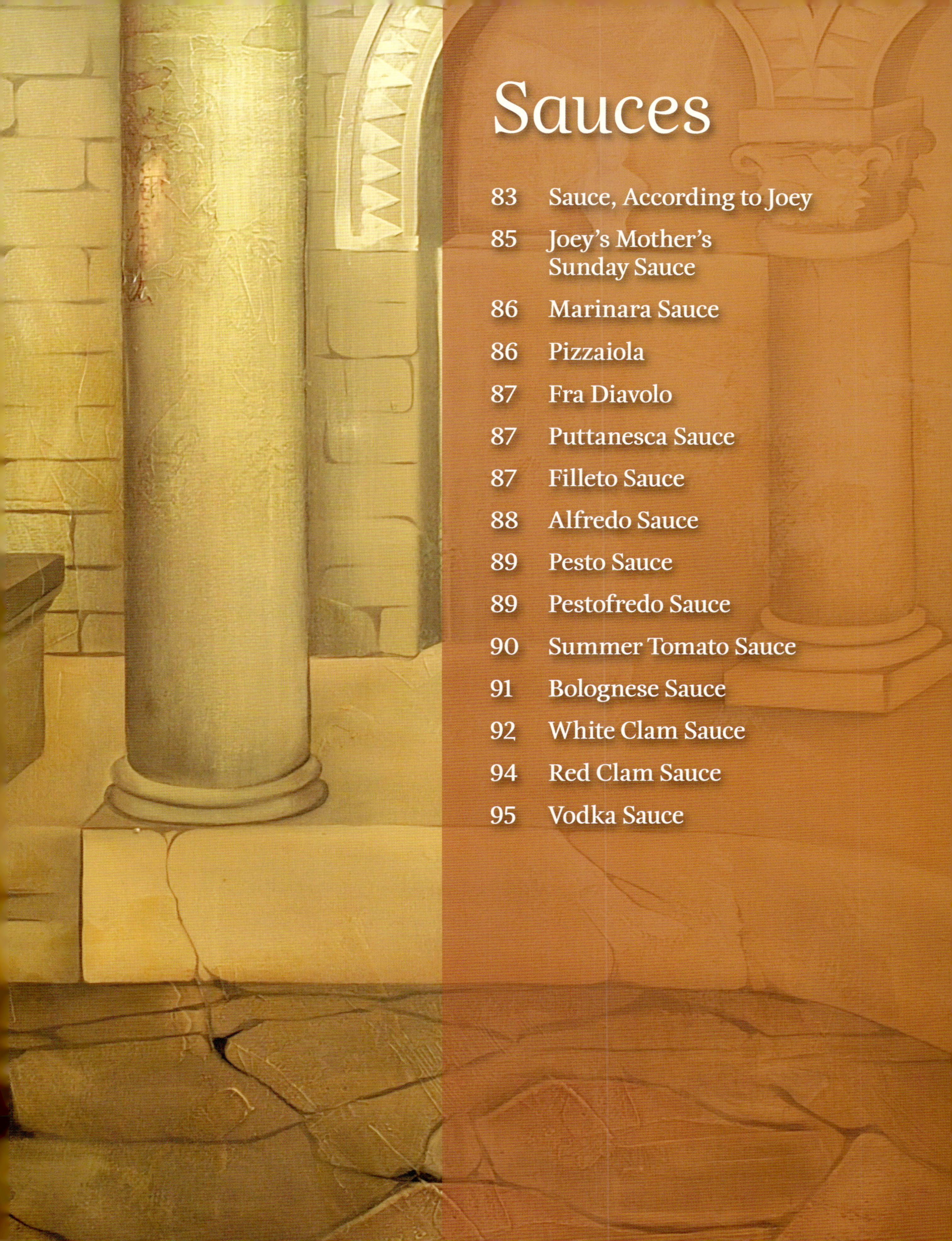

Sauces

Sauce, According to Joey

Sauce is a loaded word in Italian-American circles. Sauce is what you do all day Sunday. Sauce is what your mother makes better than anybody else's mother. Sauce is the family secret, passed down from one generation to the next. And sauce is the glue that helps your family (and your lasagna) stick together.

In the old country, sauce—as in tomato sauce—was just one of many components of the traditional Italian table. In this country, red sauce has become shorthand for what it means to be Italian-American. At Joey's we make my mother's slow-simmered Sunday sauce at the rate of more than 40 gallons per day. Not just out of respect for my mother, but by popular demand—I can still hear echoes of my mother's half-hearted protests, "Oh Joey, it's just a normal pot of sauce".

As good as it is, my mother's is not our only sauce. The American palette has steadily evolved, and our customers now appreciate the "other" Italian sauces—sauces that reflect Italy's tremendous regional diversity. The sauces in this chapter are from all over Italy. Marinara, a quick tomato sauce, captures the fresh, vibrant flavors of the south. Bolognese, a rich meat sauce with tomato undertones, hails from Bologna in the Emilia Romagna region, which many consider to be the culinary capital of Italy. Alfredo sauce was created in Rome—and quickly embraced in the U.S.—but it reflects the Northern Italian affection for sauces rich with butter and cheese.

These diverse sauces all adhere to my credo of Italian cuisine: start with the very best ingredients and preserve their integrity. The goal is to have the original flavors shine—not to have them compete with other complicated ingredients. As my mother used to say, "The simpler the better—don't garbage the sauce with too many spices." In other words, clarity is a priority in Italian sauces.

Harmony is another key concept in Italian cuisine. A sauce should complement, not overpower, its partner. Here's where the cook plays choreographer, finding just the right balance of flavors and textures.

And finally, this book isn't a bible, and the recipes aren't gospels. It's great to learn the basics but don't be afraid to express your inner chef. Italian cooking is pretty forgiving, as long as you use top-quality ingredients and common sense. When I cook, I throw in a handful of this, a pinch of that, and a little more of whatever makes sense. Cooking is a combination of science and art, so feel free to be creative!

A Tip from Joey

At Joey's we don't serve pasta swimming in sauce, nor do we slap the sauce on top of the pasta. The two partners need to be briefly introduced before they are served.
Here's how we do it: In a saucepan, we combine about 1 cup of cooked pasta, 1 tablespoon of butter (to help carry the flavor), then 1/4 cup of sauce, and a sprinkle of grated cheese.
Over low heat, we stir everything together, gently but thoroughly. To serve, we slip the pasta into shallow bowls and crown it with a little more sauce.

A Tip from Joey

You may be tempted to control the splatter by covering your sauce as it simmers. But all that trapped heat turns the sauce a dark red color and gives it a burnt taste. Better to wipe up the mess than spoil the sauce. Or purchase a splatter screen, which allows the heat to escape and catches most of the splatter. Better yet, use a really large stockpot, capable of holding 2 to 3 gallons or more, keep your heat consistently low, and stir the sauce every chance you get.

Joey's Mother's Sunday Sauce

For as long as I can remember, my mother spent Sundays at the stove, stirring this perfectly balanced, deeply flavored sauce, and probably praying for patience, as the six of us kids ran circles around her. I still feel her love when I taste this sauce.

Makes about 5 quarts—to make a smaller batch, just cut the ingredient amounts in half

1 pound	pork butt, left whole
	Salt and pepper, to taste
½ cup	olive oil
2 ounces	salt pork, sliced 1-inch thick
1 pound	chuck steak, well marbled, left whole
1 pound	Italian sausage links, sweet or hot
1 cup	diced onion
5	cloves garlic, minced
2 (6-ounce)	cans tomato paste
1 cup	red wine, such as Chianti
5 (28-ounce)	cans crushed tomatoes in *heavy* purée
½	bunch fresh basil, julienned
	Pinch dried basil
1 ½ tablespoons	salt
	Freshly ground pepper
2 cups	water

Lightly season the pork butt and steak with salt and pepper. In a 16-quart, heavy-bottomed stockpot, heat the oil over medium-high heat. Add the pork butt, salt pork, and chuck steak and cook for 10 minutes, turning to brown evenly on all sides. Add the sausage and brown but do not cook through. Remove all meat and set aside.

Reduce heat to medium. Add the onions and garlic and cook, without browning, until soft and translucent, about 5 minutes. Blend the tomato paste into the onions and garlic. Increase heat to medium high, add wine, and cook for about 3 minutes, to cook off the alcohol. Stir in the crushed tomatoes, fresh and dried basil, salt, and pepper. Add the water and bring to a boil. Immediately reduce heat to low and return the salt pork, pork butt, sausage, and chuck steak to sauce. Simmer the sauce, uncovered, for 2 to 3 hours, stirring occasionally, or until the pork and chuck steak are almost falling-apart. Remove all of the meat from the sauce. Serve the meat separately; family style on a platter, or chop the meat and return to the sauce for a Bolognese style sauce.

To serve the sauce immediately with pasta: in a large serving bowl, thoroughly mix 4 cups of cooked pasta with 3 tablespoons of butter, then 2 cups of warm sauce and 1/4 cup of grated Romano or 3 tablespoons of Parmigiano-Reggiano cheese. Top with additional sauce and serve.

If you are not using the sauce immediately, cool it to room temperature and refrigerate in an airtight container for up to 1 week. When ready to serve the sauce, transfer to a saucepan and heat very slowly over low heat, stirring frequently. Do not let the sauce boil or burn. If the sauce is too thick, add a small amount of water after it is thoroughly reheated.

Marinara Sauce

Sometimes simpler is better. This tomato sauce has a fresh tomato flavor and a chunkier texture than the slow-simmered Sunday sauce. Marinara sauce is great solo or as a base for the lively variations that follow.

Makes about 3 quarts

⅓ cup	olive oil
6 ounces	salt pork left whole or pancetta, coarsely chopped
1 cup	coarsely chopped onion
4	cloves garlic, finely chopped
3 (28-ounce)	cans Italian plum tomatoes in juice, San Marzano variety preferred
½ cup (4 ounces)	tomato paste
½ cup	water, to rinse tomato paste can
½ bunch	fresh basil, coarsely chopped
1 teaspoon	dried basil
2 teaspoons	salt
1 teaspoon	black pepper

In a medium saucepan, heat the olive oil over medium–high heat and brown the salt pork or pancetta. Add the onions and garlic and cook, without browning, until soft and translucent. Place the tomatoes in a bowl, squeeze tomatoes through your fingers, and add to the pot. Stir in the tomato paste. Fill the tomato paste can with water, swirl it around to get all the paste and pour it into the saucepan. Add the basil, salt, and pepper. Bring to a boil and cook for 5 minutes. Reduce heat and simmer, uncovered, for 45 minutes, stirring occasionally. Remove salt pork.

Pizzaiola

Not exactly a salsa, but a bit thick to technically be a sauce, pizzaiola makes a great topping for steaks, burgers, or grilled chicken. If you prefer a thinner consistency, just add more Marinara; if you prefer it chunkier, add less. Feel free to be creative and add or substitute your favorite ingredients, such as capers, olives, or hot peppers. Just let your taste buds be your guide.

1	green bell pepper, stemmed, seeded, sliced into ¼-inch strips
1	red bell pepper, stemmed, seeded, sliced into ¼-inch strips
1	medium onion, sliced into ¼-inch strips
1 cup	sliced or quartered fresh mushrooms, washed
1 tablespoon	butter
1 tablespoon	olive oil
1 cup	Marinara Sauce (see above)

In a medium sauté pan over medium heat, melt the butter, then add the olive oil. Increase the heat to medium-high, then add the peppers and onion and sauté until softened. Add the mushrooms and sauté until browned. Add the Marinara Sauce and heat through. To serve, spoon over the meat of your choice.

Fra Diavolo

In Italian, this means "Brother Devil," so I keep adding red pepper until the sauce is as hot as I like. Be careful the first time and taste as you go, so you don't make it too hot!

Makes 1 quart

4 cups	Marinara Sauce (page 86)
1 tablespoon	crushed red pepper flakes, for more heat add ½ teaspoon at a time, to taste and heat preference

Puttanesca Sauce

If you like your sauce hot and spicy, this is for you. Remember, you can always increase the heat by adding more hot pepper. But you can't go back, so start mild and keep tasting. Puttanesca is a hearty sauce, so it pairs well with more substantial pasta, such as spaghetti, fettuccini, rigatoni, or penne.

Makes 1 quart

¼ cup	olive oil
4	hot cherry peppers, stemmed and chopped
3	garlic cloves, thinly sliced
3	anchovies, chopped
15	Kalamata olives, pitted and halved
½ cup	large Italian capers
¼ cup	chopped fresh basil
4 cups	Marinara Sauce (page 86)

In a large saucepan, over medium heat, combine the olive oil, peppers, garlic, anchovies, olives, capers, and basil. Sauté, stirring occasionally, for 3 minutes. Add the Marinara Sauce and bring to a simmer. Reduce the heat and cook for 10 minutes to reduce the sauce.

Filleto Sauce

Makes 1 quart

¼ cup	olive oil
3	cloves garlic, thinly sliced
1	red onion, coarsely chopped
1 cup	coarsely chopped pancetta, or ½ cup coarsely chopped prosciutto and ½ cup coarsely chopped bacon
15	Kalamata olives, pitted and halved
4 cups	Marinara Sauce (page 86)

In a saucepan over medium heat, combine the olive oil, garlic, and onion. Cook until onion is soft and translucent. Add the pancetta or prosciutto/bacon combination and sauté until lightly browned. Add the olives and Marinara Sauce and heat through.

Alfredo Sauce

Alfredo sauce was first created in Rome in 1914 by Alfredo Di Lelio. In 1927, Hollywood stars Douglas Fairbanks and Mary Pickford brought the recipe back to Los Angeles, where Alfredo sauce became a star in its own right. The original recipe for Alfredo sauce calls for Parmigiano-Reggiano, but at Joey's we prefer to use Asiago cheese for a creamier texture.

Makes 1 quart

4 cups	**heavy cream**
8 tablespoons	**butter, cut into pieces**
2 cups	**grated Asiago cheese**

In a large saucepan, combine the cream and the butter over medium heat, keeping a close eye on it—you want it to reach the point just before it starts to boil. (If allowed to boil, you run the risk of the cream separating. Once it has separated, there is no going back; you will be starting over or making a different sauce.)

When you see tiny bubbles begin to form on the edges of the pan, immediately reduce heat to low and let simmer for a few minutes.

When sauce has reduced and thickened slightly, add cheese and stir until Asiago has melted into the sauce. Toss the sauce with your favorite pasta and serve immediately. I recommend fresh fettuccine (pages 100-101).

Pesto Sauce

Pesto simply means "paste" in Italian. This dense sauce, which originated in Genoa, is essentially a paste with fresh basil as the key component. One of the advantages of pesto is that proportions don't have to be precise. You can increase or decrease ingredients to alter the flavor and texture. It's fun to experiment—but I still prefer pesto with basil in the starring role!

Makes about 1 ½ cups

2 cups	**tightly packed fresh basil leaves, stems removed**
¼ cup	**pignoli, or pine nuts, lightly toasted**
4	**cloves fresh garlic**
½ cup	**olive oil**
½ cup	**grated Romano cheese**

Wash and dry the basil leaves and remove any thick stems. In a food processor, grind the basil leaves, pine nuts, and garlic while slowly drizzling in the olive oil. When thoroughly blended, add the cheese.

To use immediately, toss about ¾ cup pesto with 1 pound of your favorite cooked pasta, using just enough sauce to lightly coat the pasta. Some pastas such as cappellini, or angel hair will call for adding a bit more pesto to coat the pasta. Pesto is also great on pizza, tossed with roasted potatoes, spread on toasted bread, or mixed into scrambled eggs.

To store in the refrigerator, transfer the pesto to an airtight container and cover with a layer of olive oil to prevent discoloration. Use within 1 week. Pesto also freezes well packed in an airtight container—but without the layer of oil.

Pestofredo Sauce

Mix Pesto Sauce in equal parts with Alfredo Sauce (page 88) to make a sauce I call Pestofredo. At Joey's, this blend of creamy Alfredo and vibrant Pesto has become one of our most popular sauces.

Tips from Joey

Once you grasp the concept of pesto, you can experiment with other ingredients and create your own signature pesto. Try sun-dried tomatoes or artichoke hearts instead of basil; walnuts or almonds instead of pine nuts; or Parmigiano-Reggiano or Asiago instead of Romano cheese.

To maximize the flavor of pignoli, or pine nuts, lightly toast them, either in a dry skillet over medium-high heat or on a baking sheet in a 225 degree F oven. Be very careful when toasting—pine nuts have a high oil content and burn very quickly. Toast just until they begin to give off their aroma, then immediately remove from heat and set aside to cool.

Summer Tomato Sauce

In my book, ripe tomatoes—still warm from the sun—are the essence of summer. This simple sauce cooks in a flash, so you can go from garden (or your local farmers' market) to table in no time. I prefer Roma tomatoes for my summer sauce—they have fewer seeds, a more meaty texture, and a really rich flavor. I like to pair this light sauce with a slender pasta such as spaghetti, linguine, or cappellini. For a sublime summer experience, make fresh fettuccini (pages 100–101) and toss it lightly with the Summer Tomato Sauce and freshly grated Parmigiano-Reggiano.

Makes about 6 cups or 1 ½ quarts

3 quarts	**water**
24	**medium Roma tomatoes—right off the vine, if possible!**
¼ cup	**extra virgin olive oil**
4	**cloves garlic, thinly sliced**
1	**small onion, coarsely chopped**
½ cup (4 ounces)	**tomato paste**
10	**fresh basil leaves, stems removed, chopped**
	Salt and black pepper, to taste

In a stockpot, bring the water to a boil. Have a large bowl of ice water nearby. Score the bottom of each tomato with an "x." Slip the scored tomatoes into the boiling water and boil for 2 minutes, or until the skins start to crack open. Transfer the tomatoes to the ice water. When cool enough to handle, remove the skin by gently squeezing each tomato—the "x" slit will help the skin slide off easily.

In a saucepan, heat the olive oil over medium-high heat. Add the garlic and onion and cook, without browning, until soft and translucent. Stir in the tomato paste and reduce heat. Lightly squeeze the tomatoes through your fingers and into the pot. Add the basil and increase heat to medium high. Bring to a boil, then reduce heat to low and simmer for 20 to 30 minutes. The longer you cook the sauce, the thicker it becomes. Season with salt and pepper.

Bolognese Sauce

As kids we called this meat sauce, which says it all. To get rich, meaty flavor, you need meat with a little fat. I know it's politically incorrect to say this—in our health-conscious culture—but you don't get much flavor from very lean meat. Here's my solution: make your sauce with some nice, marbled meat, then take a brisk walk after dinner.

Makes about 1 ½ quarts

¼ cup	olive oil
1	onion, coarsely chopped
2	cloves garlic, minced
1 pound	Italian pork sausage—loose or casing removed
1 pound	ground beef, 80% lean
¾ cup (6 ounces)	tomato paste
1 cup (8 ounces)	tomato purée
2 (28-ounce)	cans crushed tomatoes in heavy purée
½ cup	water
1 teaspoon	salt
1 teaspoon	ground pepper
1 cup	chopped fresh parsley or fresh basil

In a large, heavy-bottomed saucepan, heat the oil over medium-high heat. Add the onions and garlic and cook slowly, without browning, until onions are soft and translucent, and garlic is fragrant. Add the sausage and brown for 5 minutes, breaking sausage apart with a wooden spoon. Add the beef and brown until meat is no longer pink. Stir the tomato paste into meat and cook for 3 minutes.

Add the tomato purée, tomatoes, water, salt, pepper, and parsley and bring to a boil. Immediately reduce heat to a simmer and cook sauce, stirring occasionally, for 30 minutes.

A Tip from Joey

Traditionally, Bolognese Sauce is made with the Big Three: ground beef, pork sausage, and ground veal. At Joey's, we use such a robust sausage that it would overpower the delicate veal. So we don't use veal in our Bolognese Sauce. If you miss the veal, you can always add it.

White Clam Sauce

Given my obsession with quality ingredients, it's no surprise that I recommend absolutely fresh clams, in the shell, for this sauce. The next best option is frozen, whole clams, either littleneck or baby. My final option is canned, whole, baby clams packed in their own juice. If you are using fresh clams—and I sure hope you are—buy a few extras and be sure they are all tightly closed, which means they are still alive. Before cooking, discard any clams that have opened, even slightly. At Joey's, we always use fresh clams and serve them in the shells for maximum visual impact!

Serves 4

1 cup	**water**
1 cup	**sherry or white wine**
48	**littleneck clams in the shell, or 2 cups frozen, thawed and drained baby clams, or 2 cups canned baby clams in juice, drained**
¼ cup	**olive oil**
4	**whole anchovies, canned or fresh, coarsely chopped**
4	**cloves garlic, minced**
¼ cup	**finely chopped fresh Italian parsley**
2 tablespoons	**butter**
2 cups (16 ounces)	**clam juice**
1 teaspoon	**crushed red pepper flakes, optional**

If using fresh clams in their shells, scrub them thoroughly to get rid of any sand. I rinse fresh clams 3 times in cold running water or let them soak for 10 minutes before steaming.

To steam the fresh clams, place them in a large saucepan with the water and sherry or wine. Cook, covered, over medium-high heat to steam open the shells—this takes about 4 or 5 minutes. Remove the clams, still in their shells, and set aside. Pour the liquid through a coffee filter or fine sieve to remove any sand or solid particles. Reserve the cooking liquid.

When the clams have cooled, remove from shells and set aside.

In the same large saucepan, heat the oil over medium heat and sauté the garlic and anchovies until garlic is fragrant but not brown. Add the parsley, butter, and reserved or bottled clam juice. For a little zing, add crushed red pepper flakes to taste. Add the reserved, frozen or canned clams. Bring to a boil, uncovered. Reduce heat to a simmer, cover, and continue to cook for five minutes.

To serve with linguine, as we do at Joey's, cook 1 pound of linguine until just al dente, drain, and divide the pasta into 4 bowls. Ladle the sauce over the pasta without tossing— just let it seep into the linguine. (This is one of the few pasta sauces we don't toss with butter.) Serve with crusty Italian bread to soak up every drop of the delicious sauce.

Red Clam Sauce

Fresh mussels can be very successfully substituted for the clams in this sauce. Just be sure to de-beard them, scrub thoroughly to remove any sand and discard any that aren't tightly closed.

Serves 4

½ cup	water
½ cup	white wine or sherry
48	fresh littleneck clams or mussels in the shell
	or 2 cups frozen baby clams, thawed and drained
	or 2 cups canned baby clams in juice, drained
¼ cup	olive oil
2	cloves garlic, peeled and minced
3 cups	Marinara Sauce (page 86)
¼ cup	finely chopped fresh Italian parsley
½ cup	clam juice

If using fresh clams in their shells, scrub and rinse well before steaming. Place in a large saucepan, add sherry or white wine and cook, covered, over medium-high heat to steam open the shells, about 4 or 5 minutes. Remove the clams, still in their shells, and set aside. Pour the liquid through a coffee filter or fine sieve to remove any sand or solid particles. Reserve the cooking liquid. When the clams have cooled, remove from shells and set aside.

In a large saucepan over medium heat, sauté the garlic for 2 to 3 minutes, until soft but not brown. Add the reserved, frozen or canned clams, Marinara Sauce, parsley, and reserved or bottled clam juice. Bring to a boil, uncovered. Reduce heat to a simmer, cover, and continue to cook for 10 minutes.

To serve with linguine as we do at Joey's, cook 1 pound of linguine until just al dente, drain, and divide the pasta into 4 bowls. Ladle the sauce over the pasta without tossing—just let it seep into the linguine. (This is one of the few pasta sauces we don't toss with butter).

A Tip from Joey

When cooking with wine, sherry, or any alcohol, my quality code still applies. Don't use any product labeled "cooking wine" or "cooking sherry." Usually that suggests it isn't good enough to drink. If you wouldn't drink it, why would you cook with it?

Vodka Sauce

Too many cooks don't always spoil the sauce. This Italian-American collaboration takes a standard sauce to new heights. This sauce is great with any type of pasta. Just be sure to toss the sauce with your cooked pasta to coat it completely.

Makes 1 quart

4 tablespoons	butter
	Dash of ground black pepper
¼ cup	vodka
2 cups	heavy cream
2 cups	Marinara Sauce (page 86)

Melt the butter in a saucepan over medium heat. Add the black pepper. Add the vodka and, with a long-tipped lighter, ignite vodka and allow alcohol to burn off. Stir in the cream. Add the Marinara Sauce and continue to cook for 5 minutes, reducing sauce slightly.

A Tip from Joey

I highly recommend serving Vodka Sauce with a nice al-dente rigatoni. Before tossing the sauce with pasta, add 1 cup of grated Asiago but no additional butter.

Pasta

Pasta, According to Joey

To me, pasta is soul food. It's also the temptress that lured me into this crazy business. Remember Angelina, the Italian grandmother who taught me how to make fresh pasta at Grimaldi's? I've been infatuated with the process of making pasta ever since.

Pasta may be my muse, but I never envisioned my restaurant as just another spaghetti house. From day one, Joey's has been dedicated to classic fine dining, Italian style. And classically prepared pasta is our foundation. For many Americans, all pasta is created equal—it comes out of a box, dry and brittle. But at Joey's, we use fresh pasta for many of our signature dishes. We make it from scratch, using flour, eggs, and water. Italian chef and Food Network star Mario Batali says, "Fresh pasta and dried pasta are as different as night and day." Amen. Each has its advantages. The delicacy of fresh pasta is legendary. But dried pasta also has its virtues: it is far more durable, and it's my first choice when I want pasta that is firm to the bite—*al dente*—when paired with a clam sauce, meat sauce, or chunky tomato sauce.

In Southern Italy, dried pasta is generally preferred for heartier sauces, such as my mother's Sunday sauce. In Northern Italy, where butter often replaces olive oil, handmade fresh pasta is more compatible with the region's elegant cream sauces.

At Joey's, we celebrate both traditions. As you use this cookbook, you will not be disappointed if you stick to recipes that recommend dried pasta. It's made into more than a hundred varieties, with endearing names, like ziti (little bridegrooms), tagliardi (little mops), and strozzapretti (strangle the priest). Okay, some names are not so endearing. But the umbrella word macaroni comes from the Italian phrase "Ma che carini!" which means, "My! What little dears!"

I hope that my recipes for dried pasta dishes will inspire you to try making fresh pasta. It's not difficult. It takes a little time (Under an hour, at first, then less and less time with practice. In Joey's kitchen we say, "If you have 10 minutes and two hands, you can make pasta."). But I won't lie to you, there are downsides to making fresh pasta. First, it's addictive—to make, and to eat. Second, you may not be able to handle the adulation of those who consume your plump ravioli and delicate strands of fettuccine. Seriously, making pasta from scratch will take your cooking to a new level. Don't say I didn't warn you.

Some mornings at Joey's, I run around in circles, putting out fires, trying to make decisions, taking deliveries, and answering the ever-ringing phone (not to mention trying to get this cookbook out of my head and onto the page!). In the middle of it all, one of my managers will call me over and say, "Joey, can you make me a lunch special?" I sigh, making a big show of annoyance at yet another interruption. But secretly, I am grateful for any excuse to make pasta.

Maybe it should be some little ravioli filled with prosciutto and cheese? I know we have some nice goat cheese in the cooler. Or maybe a cream sauce, with sun-dried tomatoes? Soon I am wrist-deep in flour, mixing and kneading the pasta dough, then feeding it, over and over, through the rollers of our hand-cranked pasta machine, until the sheets are so sheer that I can see the knuckles of my hands beneath them . . . did someone say special?

Whether you are preparing dried or fresh pasta, I highly recommend that you read the primer on cooking pasta (page 102). There's a little more to it than just boiling water. My simple pointers will make a big difference in your final dishes.

Fresh Pasta Dough—Basic Recipe and Technique

Truth be told, I would rather make pasta than eat pasta. For me, it is relaxing, even therapeutic. And trust me, you don't need a big work surface or a lot of expensive equipment. All you need are flour, eggs, and an inexpensive, hand-cranked pasta machine, available at any kitchen supply store.

Makes about 1 ½ pounds pasta dough—4 to 6 servings of most pasta varieties

¼ pound	all-purpose white flour
¾ pound	semolina
1	egg
¾ cup	cold water

A Tip from Joey

At Joey's, we make our fresh pasta to a ratio of three parts semolina to one part flour. This combination makes a nice toothy pasta, but, the dough is stiff and hard to manage. For a softer more elastic dough—which works better with most home pasta machines—use a higher ratio of flour to semolina, or eliminate the semolina entirely.

If you are using both flour and semolina whisk them together in a large bowl. In a separate bowl, lightly whisk the egg. Mound the flour on a clean, dry work surface and form a deep well in the center. Pour the whisked egg into the center of the well. Using your fingers, very gradually mix the egg into the flour and blend. Then add cold water 2 tablespoons at a time until the dough is smooth.

Flour your hands, gather the dough into a ball, and knead until smooth and elastic, about 5 to 10 minutes. If the dough feels dry, add a little cold water. If it feels sticky, add a little flour. Cover the dough with plastic wrap and set aside to rest for 10 to 30 minutes.

Once the dough has rested, flatten it into a disc and cut into 4 equal pieces. Working with 1 piece at a time, flatten the dough into a 6-inch square. (Wrap and refrigerate the pieces you're not using immediately.)

Set a pasta machine set on the widest setting. Holding the flattened dough in one hand, and turning the crank with the other hand, slowly guide the dough through the rollers. As it comes through the other side, catch the dough with your hand held flat, to prevent accidental tearing. Gently fold the rolled dough in half, dust very lightly with flour, and continue to roll the same piece of dough—short end first—until the desired thickness is reached. Each time you pass the dough through the rollers, adjust the dial to a lower setting. Sprinkle the dough with flour whenever it threatens to stick.

The final thickness of the dough will depend on the variety of pasta. The settings on pasta machines vary, so experiment to find your ideal setting.

Most pasta machines come with attachments for cutting the pasta into basic shapes such as fettucine or linguine once the dough is rolled out. There are also some pasta machines that are "extruders" that push the dough through metal dies for creating shapes such as orchiette, ziti, spaghetti and more. You don't have to use the attachments to cut basic pasta. Many pasta shapes can be done quickly by hand with little effort.

Once you have rolled the pasta dough out to your desired thickness, lay the pasta dough out lengthwise, then lightly dust the top of the pasta sheet with a small amount of flour or semolina (to keep the dough from sticking). Cut the pasta sheets at the desired length, about 10 to 12 inches long for shapes such as fettucine or linguine. One at a time, gently roll up the pasta sheets lengthwise. With a clean, dry and sharp knife cut across the roll in the desired width of the pasta you want, about 1/4 to 1/2 inch wide for fettucine, 1/8 inch wide for linguine, 1/2 to 1 inch for broad flat pasta such as pappardelle. Don't worry about making each of your cuts the exact width. There are many times I prefer the rustic look of hand cut pasta over machine cut pasta.

Once you have sliced through the pasta dough roll, gently unroll the cut pasta so that you have strands of pasta. I like to form single portion "nests" of fresh pasta which makes it easier to cook exactly as much as needed, and helps prevent the fresh pasta from clumping together.

Cooking Pasta, According to Joey

An old proverb says a watched pot never boils. But when you're cooking pasta, it pays to keep a close watch. There is a very short window between perfectly cooked and overcooked pasta. The ideal texture is al dente—Italian for 'to the tooth.' At this point, the pasta is tender with a little bite at the center. Overcooked pasta is soft, sticky and not worth serving.

Here is my system for cooking perfect pasta:

1. Bring a big pot of water to a full, rolling boil. I use an 8-quart pot and at least 4 quarts of water. Pasta needs plenty of water in order to roll around and expand as it cooks. The water also dilutes the starch released during cooking.

2. Add salt to the boiling water—at least one tablespoon of salt per pound of pasta. Use more salt, if you like, but no less. Pasta is generally made without salt, so it's now or never. Even a great sauce can't compensate for bland pasta.

3. Do not add oil to the cooking water. Oil may prevent the pasta from sticking together, but it also prevents the sauce from adhering to the pasta.

4. Add pasta to the boiling water and give it a good stir

5. Cover the pot while the water returns to a full boil.

6. Remove the lid and continue to cook, stirring occasionally—about every 3 to 5 minutes. Cooking times vary. Dried pasta generally takes more time to cook than fresh or filled pasta. Check package directions (or fresh pasta instructions) for estimated cooking times.

7. As the pasta cooks, watch closely. When the pasta seems pliable, taste it. Is it al dente—tender on the outside yet firm to the bite? Slightly underdone is better than overdone. Drained pasta will continue to cook as it cools.

8. When pasta is al dente, drain it—***pronto***—in a colander. Shake gently but do not remove all the water. A little surface moisture will prevent sticking and help the sauce adhere.

9. Finally, do not rinse the drained pasta. The starch on its surface will help the sauce adhere.

10. *Capice?*

Too soft? If the pasta is on the verge of overdone when you test it, quickly add a cup of cold water to the cooking water. This will slow down cooking that continues after draining. If the pasta is just plain mush, it's too late. You can slow the cooking process, but you can't shift it into reverse. Toss the pasta into the trash, start over, and keep a closer watch this time.

Too hard? If the drained pasta still tastes slightly raw, return to the empty pot. Cover the pasta with very hot water, place the pot over medium heat, cook for 3 to 5 minutes. Taste for doneness—if done, drain.

More Pasta Tips From Joey

- *Fresh pasta* cooks much faster than dried pasta, so finish your sauce first. Then follow the preceding steps to the second boil. Pay close attention. Fresh pasta will be ready to test in a flash—after 30 to 60 seconds for fine noodles such as spaghetti, or after 1 or 2 minutes for thicker varieties such as fettuccine.
- *Filled pasta*, such as ravioli, must be boiled gently—with room to spare—in order to avoid tearing the pasta and losing its filling.
- *Frozen pasta* takes a little longer to cook. Check package instructions.
- *Specialty pasta*, such as whole wheat or buckwheat pasta, may have a different texture and require a different cooking time. Ditto for flavored pasta such as spinach or tomato. We don't make or serve these varieties at Joey's. I prefer the blank canvas of classic pasta, which allows the sauce to be the star of the show.

Joey's House Filling for Ravioli

The word ravioli comes from the Genoese dialect rabiole, meaning "leftover." At Joey's, we fill ravioli with just the opposite: fresh, full-flavored, first-quality ingredients. To highlight our delicious ravioli fillings, we keep the sauce subtle—sometimes just a little butter, a whisper of fresh herbs, and a dusting of grated cheese.

Makes about 48 ravioli, or 4 first-course servings

2 cups (1 pound)	ricotta cheese
1	egg
½ cup	grated Romano cheese
½ cup	grated mozzarella cheese
¼ teaspoon	ground nutmeg
¼ cup	chopped fresh Italian parsley
	Salt and black pepper, to taste

In a medium bowl, combine all the ingredients with a large fork or spoon. Cover and refrigerate until ready to assemble.

To Fill Ravioli: Spoon the chilled filling into a pastry bag. On a clean, dry, floured surface, lay a 6 x 12-inch rectangle of pasta dough, rolled to the thinnest setting (usually #6 to #8). Using a clean metal ruler, lightly mark dough into 3-inch squares. Pipe 1 1/2 tablespoons of filling into the center of each square.

With a pastry brush, brush a line of water along the outside edges and lines between the ravioli. Cover with a second 6 x 12-inch rectangle of pasta dough. With moistened fingers, press the top layer lightly into the bottom layer along the outer edges and between ravioli. With a pastry wheel, cut the ravioli into 12 pieces. Place on a cookie sheet sprinkled with semolina. Store the ravioli in an open container in the refrigerator. Do not use foil or plastic wrap, as the pasta will stick to the foil and tear. Freeze ravioli if not cooked the same day.

To Cook Ravioli: In a large stockpot, bring 6 quarts of salted water to a boil (page 102). Using a slotted spoon, carefully add the ravioli, no more than 4 to 8 at one time. Do not crowd the ravioli, or they will stick to each other. Return the water to a boil and cook without stirring for 2 to 4 minutes—the ravioli will float to the top of the water when cooked. With a slotted spoon, carefully remove ravioli and transfer to sauce.

A Tip from Joey

While I'm a huge fan of fresh mozzarella, I definitely recommend processed mozzarella for certain recipes, such as ravioli or lasagna. Fresh mozzarella is meant to be eaten fresh, not cooked. It's too soft to grate, and it falls apart when heated. Processed mozzarella has less moisture and a dense texture, so it grates and melts perfectly. For anything that's going to be cooked or baked, use a good-quality, whole-milk, processed mozzarella.

Spinach, Prosciutto, and Goat Cheese Filling for Ravioli

A first-course serving is about 4 to 6 ravioli, a main-course serving about 6 to 8 ravioli.

Makes about 48 ravioli

2 pounds	fresh baby leaf spinach
2 tablespoons	olive oil
¼ cup	diced white onion
1	clove garlic, peeled and minced
½ cup	diced prosciutto
¼ cup	grated Asiago cheese
8 ounces	goat cheese
1 ½ pounds	fresh pasta dough (page 100)

Wash, dry, and coarsely chop spinach. In a large saucepan or skillet, heat the oil over medium-high heat. Add the onion and garlic and sauté until soft and translucent, but not browned. Add the prosciutto and sauté for 1 minute. Add the spinach and cook, stirring, until wilted. Transfer the spinach mixture to a strainer and thoroughly drain liquid. Transfer to a mixing bowl and stir in Asiago and goat cheese. Allow mixture to cool slightly, then place bowl in freezer to finish cooling and to keep the spinach bright green. Stir occasionally until completely cool, about 10 minutes. The filling should be firm and hold its shape when formed into a small ball. If it seems too wet, transfer it to strainer and press lightly to remove excess water. To fill ravioli, follow instructions on page 104.

Ravioli with Sun-Dried Tomato Alfredo Sauce

Serves 4 to 6 as a main course

48	ravioli, either Joey's House Ravioli (page 104) or Spinach, Prosciutto, and Goat Cheese Ravioli (above)
1 cup	heavy cream
¼ cup	Chicken Stock (page 54)
2 tablespoons	butter
½ cup	sun-dried tomatoes, julienned
1 cup	grated Asiago cheese
	Black pepper, to taste

In a large sauté pan, combine the cream, chicken stock, butter, and sun-dried tomatoes. Bring to a boil over medium-high heat, reduce heat to low, and simmer for 1 minute.

Meanwhile, cook the ravioli according to directions on page 104. Using a slotted spoon, carefully transfer the cooked ravioli to the sauce. Stir gently to coat the ravioli with the sauce and 1/2 cup grated Asiago.

To serve, divide the ravioli among shallow bowls, season with black pepper, and sprinkle with remaining grated Asiago.

Manicotti

The beauty of manicotti is its remarkable versatility—these large tubes of pasta can accommodate almost any filling. So feel free to personalize this recipe with chopped fresh spinach, mushrooms, cooked chicken—whatever inspires you. The delicate flavor in our classic manicotti filling is imparted by the dash of nutmeg.

Serves 4 to 6

2 cups (1 pound)	**ricotta cheese**
1	**large egg**
½ cup	**grated Romano cheese**
1 ½ cups	**grated mozzarella cheese**
¼ teaspoon	**ground nutmeg**
¼ cup	**chopped fresh Italian parsley**
	Salt and black pepper, to taste
12	**tubes dried manicotti**
3 cups	**Joey's Mother's Sunday Sauce (page 85)**

Preheat oven to 375 degrees F.

In a large pot of water, cook the manicotti until al dente, according to package directions. Drain tubes and allow to cool.

In a large mixing bowl, thoroughly combine the ricotta, egg, Romano, ½ cup mozzarella, nutmeg, parsley, and salt and pepper to taste.

When the manicotti tubes are cool enough to handle, loosely stuff them with the filling, using a spoon or pastry bag.

On the bottom of a 9 x 13-inch baking pan, spread 1 cup of the Sunday Sauce. Cover with the filled manicotti, arranged in a single layer. Pour the remaining Sunday Sauce evenly over the manicotti. Sprinkle with 1 cup of mozzarella.

Bake for 30 to 40 minutes or until the cheese starts to bubble and turn golden brown. Remove from the oven and cool for 10 minutes before serving.

Lasagna

During the Renaissance, the pope feared that the wealthy citizens of Florence were dining to excess. He set a limit of three courses per banquet, and the clever Florentines complied—with layered dishes that concealed multiple delicacies. The lasagna we serve at Joey's employs a similar strategy.

Serves 9 to 12

2 tablespoons	olive oil
1 ½ pounds	sweet or hot Italian sausage, removed from casing
1 ½ pounds	85% ground beef, lean
1	onion, chopped
1 tablespoon	minced garlic
	Salt and pepper, to taste
2 cups	Joey's Mother's Sunday Sauce (page 85)
2 pounds	ricotta cheese
1 teaspoon	granulated garlic
2	eggs
1 cup	grated Romano cheese
½ cup	minced fresh parsley
24 ounces	no-cook lasagna sheets, frozen or dried
2 cups	grated mozzarella cheese

In a large sauté pan or skillet, heat 1 tablespoon of oil over medium heat. Add the beef and sausage and brown well. Remove skillet from heat, drain excess liquid, and set skillet aside. Do not remove the meat from the skillet.

In a separate sauté pan, heat 1 tablespoon of oil over medium heat. Add the onion and minced garlic and sauté until soft and translucent, but not browned. Transfer the sautéed onion to skillet with meat mixture. Place over medium heat, and sauté for a few minutes, stirring to combine. Season with salt and pepper. Add 1 cup Sunday Sauce.

In a small bowl, combine the ricotta and eggs. Stir in the granulated garlic, 1/2 cup of the grated Romano and 6 tablespoons of the parsley.

Preheat the oven to 350 degrees F.

Layer the bottom of a large baking pan with lasagna sheets, trim to fit if necessary. Spread with half of the meat sauce. Sprinkle with 2 tablespoons Romano and 1/2 cup mozzarella.

Cover with a second layer of lasagna sheets. Spread half of the ricotta mixture over the pasta. Cover with a third layer of lasagna sheets, spread with the remaining meat sauce, and sprinkle with 2 tablespoons of Romano and 1/2 cup mozzarella.

Cover with a fourth layer of lasagna sheets. Spread with the remaining ricotta. Cover with a fifth and final layer of lasagna sheets. Spread 1 cup of Joey's Sunday sauce over pasta. Sprinkle with 1 cup mozzarella, 4 tablespoons of Romano and remaining parsley.

Bake, uncovered, for 30 to 40 minutes, until the cheese is melted and the top is lightly browned. Cut into 9 to 12 pieces and serve with additional sauce.

Fettuccine Alfredo

The original version of this classic dish calls for Parmigiano-Reggiano cheese. At Joey's, we use Asiago cheese, which also has a smooth taste and texture that I like. We can barely keep up with the orders, so I think people are more than okay with the change.

Serves 4

4 cups	**heavy cream**
8 tablespoons (4 ounces)	**butter, cut into pieces**
1 ½ pounds	**fresh fettuccine, cooked and drained (pages 100-101)**
2 cups	**grated Asiago cheese**

In a large saucepan, combine the cream and butter over medium heat. Watch the mixture closely—you do not want it to reach a boil. (If the cream is allowed to boil, it might separate. Once it has separated, there is no going back.) The second you see tiny bubbles forming on the edges of the pan, reduce the heat to low and let the mixture simmer for a few minutes.

When sauce has reduced and thickened slightly, add the drained fettuccine, then the Asiago, and toss to combine. Serve immediately.

Linguine with Chicken Livers Marinara

People either love or hate chicken livers. Personally, I love them. The key to this recipe is to ask your butcher for the freshest chicken livers available. Then cook the chicken livers in small batches (assuming you don't have a restaurant-size sauté pan) so they cook evenly.

Serves 4

¼ cup	**olive oil**
1 pound	**fresh chicken livers**
1	**small white onion, chopped**
6	**fresh mushrooms, sliced thin**
2	**cloves garlic, sliced thin**
¼ cup	**dry sherry or red wine**
2 cups	**Marinara Sauce (page 86)**
6 leaves	**fresh basil or 4 parsley sprigs, minced**
	Salt and black pepper, to taste
1 pound	**linguine, cooked according to package directions**

Drain the chicken livers in a colander, then pat them dry with paper towels. I also cut away and discard the membranes that hold the livers together, so they don't toughen up when they cook.

In a large sauté pan or skillet, heat the oil over medium-high heat. Add the chicken livers and lightly brown on all sides, about 3 to 5 minutes for medium rare. Be careful not to overcook. They should be light brown on the outside, pale pink on the inside, and creamy in texture. Remove the chicken livers from pan and set aside. Add the onion and mushrooms to the sauté pan and cook over medium-high heat until soft. Add the garlic and cook for 1 minute. Return livers to the pan, add the wine, and cook for 3 to 5 minutes to reduce the wine. Add the Marinara Sauce and basil or parsley and heat through. Serve over linguine.

Farfalle Aletea

I named this lovely yet lively dish for my beautiful daughter, Aletea. Farfalle comes from the Italian word farfalletta, which means butterfly. In the United States, we call these bowties, because they look like bowties.

Serves 4

1 pound	**farfalle (bowtie) pasta**
1 tablespoon	**olive oil**
½ cup (4 ounces)	**pancetta, chopped**
8 tablespoons	**butter**
8	**fresh mushrooms, sliced**
4 ounces	**prosciutto, sliced into ½ -inch strips**
1 (12-ounce)	**can roasted peppers packed in water, drained and chopped**
2 cups	**heavy cream**
1 cup	**frozen peas**
½ cup	**grated Asiago cheese**

In a large stockpot, cook the pasta (page 102) while preparing the sauce. In a large saucepan, heat the oil over medium heat. Add the pancetta and sauté until nicely browned. Add the butter. When melted, add the mushrooms and cook until tender. Add the prosciutto, roasted peppers, and cream. Bring to a simmer. Add the peas. Bring to a simmer, reduce heat to low.

When pasta is cooked al dente, drain well and gently stir into sauce. Add the Asiago and stir to melt.

Transfer to a large serving bowl or individual dishes and serve immediately.

Baked Stuffed Rigatoni

Rigatoni, which are pasta tubes scored with tiny ridges, make an ideal carrier for this prosciutto-studded filling and my Mom's Sunday Sauce. It takes a little time to fill these "riggies," but it's a worthwhile investment.

Makes enough for 4 to 6 servings

28	large rigatoni, or manicotti, cooked and cut into thirds
1 tablespoon	olive oil
2 cups	ricotta cheese
2	eggs
¼ cup	minced fresh parsley
1 ½ teaspoons	granulated garlic
¼ pound	sliced prosciutto, chopped
1 cup	chopped fresh spinach
	Salt and black pepper, to taste
4 cups	Joey's Mother's Sunday Sauce (page 85)
⅓ cup	grated Romano cheese
1 ½ pounds	fresh mozzarella, shredded

Cook rigatoni according to package instructions. When pasta is al dente, drain, rinse to cool, set aside. Transfer to a bowl, drizzle lightly with oil and stir gently to help prevent sticking. Cover with plastic wrap and set aside.

Preheat oven to 375 degrees F.

Ladle about 1 cup of unheated Sunday Sauce into the bottom of a 9 x 13-inch baking dish.

In a large mixing bowl, thoroughly combine the ricotta, eggs, parsley, garlic, prosciutto, and spinach. Season with salt and pepper. Transfer the filling to a pastry bag with no tip. To fill the rigatoni, carefully pipe the filling into each tube—the filling should not protrude from either end. After each "riggie" is filled, carefully transfer it to the baking pan. You will have a single layer of rigatoni.

Pour about 3/4 cup of the Sunday Sauce over the rigatoni. Use just enough sauce to coat the pasta. Sprinkle with grated Romano, followed by the shredded mozzarella.

Bake uncovered for 35 to 40 minutes, until the cheese melts and starts to bubble. If you have not used all the Sunday Sauce, ladle what remains over the pasta and return the dish to the oven for a few minutes to heat the sauce. Remove from oven and cool for 10 minutes before serving.

Stuffed "Riggies" with Vodka Sauce

Check your local Italian market for stuffed rigatoni. They are usually available frozen, but sometimes you can find them fresh in Italian delis. Prefilled with seasoned ricotta cheese, stuffed "riggies" have crimped ends to keep the cheese from leaking out. They are great with just about any sauce, but at Joey's, the most popular combination is Stuffed Rigatoni with Vodka Sauce. If you can't find stuffed rigatoni, use fresh or frozen cheese tortellini.

Makes 4 to 6 servings

2 pounds	stuffed rigatoni, with ricotta filling
6 quarts	water
4 cups	Vodka Sauce (page 95)
½ cup	grated Asiago or Parmigianno-Reggiano cheese
¼ cup	chopped fresh parsley

In a large stockpot, bring salted water to a boil. Add the rigatoni and cook according to package instructions (frozen and fresh will require different cooking times). Drain but do not rinse.

In a separate saucepan, heat the vodka sauce. Carefully transfer the rigatoni into the saucepan, toss gently to coat rigatoni thoroughly. Sprinkle with cheese and parsley. Serve immediately.

Variation: To make "Chicken Riggies," a Central New York favorite, proceed as in the recipe above but add to the Vodka Sauce: strips of cooked, boneless chicken; sautéed red and green bell peppers; and spicy hot cherry peppers. For another excellent variation, top the rigatoni with pancetta, prosciutto, or bacon that has been chopped, sautéed and crumbled.

Gnocchi

If I were to put money on the top Italian comfort foods, my trifecta would certainly include gnocchi. It's tough to compete against pasta and risotto, but homemade gnocchi—especially my tender potato gnocchi—is definitely a contender. Gnocchi should be light and fluffy, not dense and doughy. Here's my secret: if you don't over mix the cooked potatoes, they won't turn to glue.

Makes about 3 ½ pounds of gnocchi; serves 4 as an entrée, up to 8 as an appetizer

3 pounds	**Idaho baking potatoes, whole, scrubbed but not peeled**
	Salt and white pepper, to taste
1 teaspoon	**grated nutmeg**
2	**eggs, beaten**
3 cups	**flour**
1 cup	**Joey's Mother's Sunday Sauce (page 85)**
¼ cup	**Parmigiano Reggiano, grated**

In a large stockpot, cover the potatoes with water, add salt, and bring to boil. Cook for 45 minutes, or until tender. Do not pierce the potatoes, or water will seep in—and potato starch will seep out. And do not overcook, or the skins will break. Remove the potatoes from water and set aside to cool.

When cool enough to handle, use your fingers to peel away the potato skins. While still warm, put the potatoes through a food mill or ricer. Repeat. (Do not be tempted to use a mixer or food processor for this step—it will turn the potatoes to glue).

Immediately transfer the potatoes to large mixing bowl. Season with salt, pepper, and nutmeg. Create a well in the center of the potatoes. Add the eggs and lightly stir to combine. Add 2 cups of the flour. Mix gently with a spatula until the potato dough starts to hold together, like pie crust.

Begin to knead the dough while still in the bowl. Slip your fingers under the dough and flip it toward you, while gradually adding the remaining 1 cup of flour. Turn the dough onto a clean, dry, floured work surface and continue to knead until all the flour is absorbed, but the dough is still spongy and slightly wet.

Pat the dough into a large rectangle. With a pastry cutter, cut 2-inch pieces from the end of the dough. Dust the work surface with flour and roll each piece into a long cylinder, 1/2 inch in diameter. To form the individual gnocchi, cut the cylinder into 1-inch pieces.

To create grooves, gently roll each piece over the back side of fork tines (if you don't have a gnocchi board). Hold each gnocchi between your thumb and index finger. Press your thumb into the gnocchi to create an indent, then roll forward into a small cylinder. Place the finished gnocchi, in a single layer, on a tray sprinkled with cornmeal. If not using the gnocchi right away, place them in a shallow, resealable container with a little cornmeal on the bottom. Remember, do not stack the gnocchi. Freeze and use within 1 month.

To cook the gnocchi, in a large pot, bring 4 quarts of salted water to a full boil. Add the first batch of gnocchi. Do not crowd. Cook until they float to the surface. Gently remove the gnocchi with a slotted spoon and set aside. Repeat with remaining gnocchi.

Meanwhile, in a large sauté pan over medium heat, combine the Sunday Sauce and butter. Carefully add the drained gnocchi to the sauce and heat briefly. Do not stir. Instead, gently swirl the pan to coat the gnocchi with sauce. Transfer to a shallow bowl, sprinkle with Parmigiano-Reggiano. Serve immediately.

A Tip from Joey

I recommend that you purchase a "gnocchi board," which is a small wooden tool with ridges to form the gnocchi. This simple tool is modestly priced and can be found at kitchenware stores or Italian food markets.

Risotto, According to Joey

The leisurely, methodical process of making risotto certainly goes against the grain of our hectic culture, which is probably why I love to make it. With risotto, the key ingredient is patience. You can't take shortcuts, prepare it ahead, or stray from a precise list of high-quality ingredients. According to Marcella Hazan, one of my favorite Italian chefs, "The fundamental technique for making risotto is unalterable—rice cooked by another method, however good it may be, is not risotto, nor should it be so described."

But making risotto is not an elaborate, all-day affair. It takes half an hour max. To achieve the perfect, creamy consistency, you have to gently coax the starch out of the rice, through constant stirring and the very gradual addition of hot liquid. The goal is to keep each grain of rice intact and al dente—cooked, but with a little bite in the center. The variety of rice is critical, and Arborio rice is ideal: round, firm, and packed with starch. As the risotto cooks, some of that starch seeps into the sauce, while some remains in the rice, giving risotto its signature bite. Arborio rice is now widely available—look for packages marked superfino, for the plumpest, largest grains.

For those who are curious about the chemistry of cooking, the process of making risotto makes a great case study. First, the rice is gently sautéed in olive oil (usually with minced onion and garlic). It seems like a simple step, but important changes are taking place. The flavors from the onion and garlic are seeping into the rice. The olive oil is toughening the thin outer shell of the rice, but only slightly. (At this stage, it is very important that nothing be allowed to brown, so the flavors remain subtle and the color creamy white.)

In the next step, hot liquid is gradually ladled into the rice. Each addition must be fully absorbed before more liquid is added. The key here is constant stirring—remember what I said about patience? If you keep the rice moving, you'll prevent it from stewing in the hot broth and turning to mush.

Finally, when the rice is al dente—tender on the outside, slightly firm at the core—you immediately remove the risotto from the heat and enrich it with cheese—the best—quality Italian cheese you can find. Parmigiano Reggiano is traditional, but feel free to substitute grated Romano (for a saltier finish) or Asiago (for a creamier texture).

Risotto

A cross between comfort food and high culinary art, risotto is a labor of love to prepare. The finished product is addictive, and believe it or not, so is the process of making risotto. After a few tries, it becomes second nature. I actually find it therapeutic. It gives me a good excuse to slow down, sip a little wine, decompress from the day, hum, sing, meditate, or simply contemplate the genius of the Italian palate.

Serves 6 to 8

6 cups	Chicken Stock (page 54)
1 cup	white wine
3 tablespoons	butter
3 tablespoons	olive oil
1 tablespoon	chicken soup base (see page 200)
2	cloves garlic, peeled and minced
1	small onion, minced
2 cups	Arborio rice
3 tablespoons	butter
	Salt and ground pepper, to taste
1 cup	grated Parmigiano-Reggiano cheese
¼ cup	minced fresh parsley

In a deep saucepan, bring the chicken stock and chicken base to barely a simmer. Continue to simmer over very low heat.

In a heavy-bottomed, 8-quart saucepan or stockpot, over medium heat, melt the butter with the oil. Add the garlic and onion and gently sauté for about 3 minutes. (This allows the garlic and onion to slowly release their flavors into the risotto without dominating the other ingredients.) Add the wine and simmer for 1 to 2 minutes to cook off the alcohol.

Add the rice and stir for about 3 minutes or until the rice is coated with oil. Do not allow the rice to brown. Increase the heat to medium-high and add 1 cup of the hot chicken stock, stirring constantly until it is completely absorbed by the rice.

Immediately add another cup of hot stock, stirring constantly. Continue to add stock, a little at a time, stirring constantly, until the rice reaches a creamy consistency. Taste as you go; rice should be al dente but not hard or chewy.

When the texture suits your taste, remove pan from heat, add the butter, and stir thoroughly into the rice. Season with salt and pepper. Stir in the grated Parmigiano-Reggiano. Ladle into shallow bowls, garnish with the parsley, and serve immediately.

Variations Risotto is wonderful solo, but it's also a perfect base for ingredients such as asparagus, mushrooms, peas, shrimp, or chicken. I prefer to keep it simple—with one or maybe two extra ingredients—so the individual flavors and textures stand out. After the risotto is finished cooking—and just before serving—gently stir in the extra ingredients, such as:

Asparagus: steamed or blanched asparagus stalks that have been submerged in an ice bath, then sliced into bite-size pieces.

Mushrooms: whole or sliced mushrooms that have been sautéed for 2 to 3 minutes in a little olive oil.

Peas: fresh peas, if possible, which have been shelled and blanched.

Sun-Dried Tomatoes: added at the last moment, so they won't turn the risotto pink.

Shrimp: peeled and deveined shrimp that have been steamed or sautéed.

Chicken: boneless, skinless chicken that has been sautéed or oven roasted and cut into bite-size pieces.

Arancini with Gorgonzola

In the unlikely event that you have leftover risotto, treat yourself to the delicacy known as arancini, which are deep-fried rice balls with a surprise burst of Gorgonzola in the center. Another option for leftover risotto is to flatten it into small pancakes and sauté on both sides until crisp and golden brown.

Makes about 8 to 12 arancini balls

2 cups	**cold Risotto (plain or variation page 120)**
1 cup (8 ounces)	**Gorgonzola cheese**
1 cup	**Seasoned Bread Crumbs (page 201)**
2	**eggs, lightly beaten**
4 cups	**vegetable oil**
¼ cup	**grated Romano cheese**
1 cup	**Marinara Sauce (page 86)**

For each Arancini, form a small handful of risotto into a flat circle about 3 inches in diameter and 1/2 inch thick. Tuck a teaspoon of Gorgonzola in the center of each circle and wrap the risotto around the cheese, forming a ball. Dip the ball in the eggs, then roll in the bread crumbs until evenly coated.

In a deep, heavy skillet, heat the oil to 350 degrees F.

Carefully slip the rice balls into the hot oil. Do not crowd, or they will stick together.

Fry until golden brown. Remove with a slotted spoon, drain on paper towels, top with Romano and serve immediately with marinara sauce for dipping.

46
COPPIE

Beef, Lamb Pork & Veal

A Tip from Joey

To store cooked meatballs, without sauce, transfer them to a sealed container and store for up to 1 week in the refrigerator. Reheat the meatballs with sauce on the stove or in an oven at 200 degrees F. Meatballs—fresh or reheated—should be cooked to an internal temperature of 165 degrees F. If you don't have a meat thermometer, take a meatball from the middle of your batch and cut it half. It should be evenly cooked throughout, with no pink in the center.

Joey's Meatballs

I was genuinely honored to be crowned the 2006 Meatball King of Central New York, and the trophy was proudly displayed in the bar at Joey's. We take great pride in our meatballs, and I'm happy to share the title—and the recipe—with our customers.

Makes about 12 large meatballs

For Joey's Meatball Mix

1 pound	ground beef, 80% lean
1 pound	ground pork
2	eggs
½ cup	grated Romano cheese
1	small yellow onion, diced
2 tablespoons	chopped fresh Italian parsley
1 cup	Seasoned Bread Crumbs (page 201)
1 tablespoon	granulated garlic
½ teaspoon	salt
½ teaspoon	black pepper
¼ cup	cold water
½ cup	Olive Oil Blend (page 198)
3 quarts	Joey's Mother's Sunday Sauce (page 85)

Using your hands, combine the ground beef and pork in a large mixing bowl. Add the eggs, Romano, onion, parsley, bread crumbs, garlic, salt, and pepper. Add the water a little at a time. Continue to mix by hand until everything is evenly blended. The mixture should be moist and hold its shape without crumbling.

I use an ice-cream scoop to form meatballs that weigh 3 to 4 ounces each, before cooking. (Keeping the size uniform helps them cook evenly.) If you prefer to roll the meatballs by hand, have a small bowl of water nearby to moisten your palms as you work.

When all meatballs are formed, cover the bottom of a heavy skillet with 1/4-inch oil and heat to medium high. Add the meatballs but do not crowd—they should not touch each other. Brown the meatballs on all sides, turning as they brown (about 10 minutes total cooking time).

In a large sauce pot, over low heat, bring 3 quarts of Sunday Sauce to a simmer. Add the meatballs and continue to simmer gently for 30 minutes. Serve the meatballs with sauce, with pasta, as a sandwich, or simply solo: *"Sometimes the meatball likes to be alone."* I love this line from *Big Night*, the film in which two Italian brothers prepare an extravagant meal at their modest Italian restaurant. There is nothing illegal about serving a solo meatball, crowned simply with grated cheese.

Italian-Style Filet Mignon

When I was in Italy, I ordered a steak prepared Tuscan-style. It made me homesick for this signature dish from Joey's. For this recipe, feel free to substitute sirloin, rib-eye, or your favorite cut for the filet.

Serves 4

2 pounds	filet mignon, cut into 4 (8-ounce) pieces
1 teaspoon	olive oil
4	cloves garlic, peeled and minced
4 tablespoons	butter
1 cup	red wine, Chianti preferred
	Salt and pepper to taste
¼ cup	chopped fresh basil or parsley

Preheat broiler or prepare grill.

Cook the filets to about 75 percent done. Remove from heat and set aside.

Add the oil to a large skillet and heat to medium-high. Add the filets and sear for 2 minutes on each side. Transfer to serving plates while preparing sauce. Add the garlic to the skillet and sauté for 1 minute or until soft. Add the wine and cook until the alcohol evaporates. (Or you may add the wine, ignite it with a long-tip lighter to flambé, and allow to burn until the flame is extinguished.)

Add the butter to the skillet and allow it to melt. Lower heat to medium and reduce the sauce for 3 minutes, stirring constantly. Season with salt and pepper and pour sauce over the reserved filets. Garnish with the parsley or basil.

A Tip from Joey

Give It a Rest. Don't worry about your steaks getting cold while you make the sauce. Any meat benefits from a short rest between cooking and serving—depending on the thickness of the steak, 8 to 10 minutes. The steak actually continues cooking as it rests. Be sure to use the juice released by the steak—it's loaded with great flavor! Add it to the sauce or pour it over the steak just before serving.

Beef Braciola

I like to make Beef Braciola while my Sunday Sauce simmers, timing it so they meet in the sauce for the final 45 minutes—just enough time for the flavors to merge beautifully.

Serves 4

Sauce	
1 quart	**Joey's Mother's Sunday Sauce (page 85)**
Braciola	
1 pound	**top round beef, cut into 8 slices, each ⅛-inch thick**
	Salt and black pepper
½ pound	**Joey's Meatball Mix (page 125)**
8	**slices provolone cheese, domestic preferred for its melting quality**
½ cup	**grated Romano cheese**
4	**eggs, hard-boiled**
½ cup	**chopped fresh parsley**

Preheat oven to 350 degrees F.

For each serving arrange 2 slices of beef edge-to-edge on a clean, dry cutting board. Using a mallet, gently pound the beef into one rectangle, with a short side closest to you. Season with salt and pepper. Spread a thin layer of meatball mixture over the rectangle, keeping 1 inch clear at edges. Cover with 2 slices of provolone and sprinkle lightly with Romano. Chop the eggs and spread over each rectangle. Sprinkle with the parsley.

Starting at the shorter, lower end of the rectangle, fold the uncovered border inward over the filling. Then roll the beef into a cylinder, applying pressure to help everything compress and adhere. As you roll the beef, turn the uncoated borders in to seal the edges.

To keep the rolls intact while cooking, wrap securely in foil: Place a 10 x 12-inch sheet of aluminum foil diagonally on work surface. Position a beef cylinder above the lower point of the foil and roll forward, tucking excess foil inward. Arrange the sealed cylinders in a 10 x 12-inch baking dish and pour 1/2 cup water into bottom of dish. Bake for 45 minutes—the internal temperature of the braciola should be 165 degrees F. Remove from oven and cool to room temperature. Do not remove foil until the rolls are completely cool and firm.

Carefully add the braciola to simmering Sunday Sauce and cook for 30 to 45 minutes. To keep the braciola intact, be gentle when stirring the sauce.

Serve braciola either whole or sliced over your favorite pasta. Ladle some extra Sunday sauce over the Braciola and pasta, garnish with parsley.

Braised Lamb Shanks

Ask your butcher to cut these shanks from the hindquarter of the lamb, which is naturally more tender.

Serves 4

2 quarts	Beef Stock (page 55) or Veal Stock (page 54)
1 (24-ounce)	can whole plum tomatoes (preferably San Marzano)
½ cup	flour
½ teaspoon	salt
½ teaspoon	ground black pepper
4	lamb shanks, about 22 ounces each
½ cup	Olive Oil Blend (page 198)
1 tablespoon	fresh rosemary
2	medium carrots, diced
4	stalks celery, diced
1	Spanish onion, diced
4	cloves garlic, peeled and minced
½ cup	red wine, preferably Chianti
¼ cup	chopped fresh basil
2 tablespoons	cornstarch

In a large skillet or saucepan, bring the beef or veal stock to a simmer over medium high heat. Add the tomatoes and return to a simmer.

In a shallow bowl, combine the flour, salt, and pepper. Roll each lamb shank in flour mixture to coat all sides. In a heavy skillet or Dutch oven, heat the oil over medium-high heat. Add the lamb shanks and brown on all sides, about 10 to 15 minutes. Transfer the lamb shanks to a large baking dish at least 4 inches deep. Position the shanks upright, using the flat side of the bone as the base. Sprinkle with the rosemary and set aside.

Drain the skillet, leaving a thin coat of oil in the bottom. Return skillet to medium-high heat and add the carrots, celery, and onion. Sauté for 3 to 4 minutes, stirring constantly to scrape up any browned bits of flour. Add the garlic and sauté for 1 minute. Add the red wine and cook off the alcohol. Add the basil and 1 quart of the hot beef or veal stock. Simmer for 20 minutes to reduce.

Preheat oven to 375 degrees F.

Pour the remaining quart of hot stock into the pan with the lamb shanks. Add the reduced stock and vegetables from the skillet, cover tightly, and bake for 3 hours. Remove from the oven and skim excess fat from the top. To thicken the sauce, thoroughly blend 2 tablespoons cornstarch with 2 tablespoons cold water in a small bowl. Gently stir into the sauce.

Allow the lamb shanks and sauce to rest for 15 minutes before serving over garlic mashed potatoes (my personal favorite), noodles, or rice.

Pork Loin Roast

This roast is so simple you could make it in your sleep—and so special you could serve it to a king. After decades of watching food trends come and go, I have learned that simplicity never goes out of style.

Serves 4 to 6

4 pounds	**center-cut pork loin**
1 cup	**white wine**
4 cloves	**garlic, halved**
¼ cup	**olive oil**
1	**sprig fresh rosemary**
½	**fresh lemon**
	Salt and black pepper to taste

Preheat the oven to 350 degrees F.

Rinse the pork loin and pat dry with paper towels. Pour the wine into the bottom of a roasting pan and add the pork, fat side up. With a small, pointed knife, make 8 slits, about 3/4-inch deep, in the pork. Insert the garlic halves into the slits. Drizzle the olive oil over pork. Strip the rosemary leaves from the sprig and sprinkle over meat. Squeeze the lemon juice over pork and season with salt and pepper.

Place pan in oven and roast for 20 minutes per pound. (A 4-pound roast will take about 1 hour and 20 minutes.) The internal temperature should reach 160 degrees F when done. Remove pork from oven and allow to rest for 20 minutes before carving.

Serve the pork with pan juices and Rosemary Roasted Potatoes (page 74), which can be added to the oven about 40 minutes before the meat is done

A Tip from Joey

Today's pork is not the same pork my mother bought 20 years ago. Modern farming and low-fat thinking mean that pork is increasingly lean. This is good if you're watching your fat-intake, not so good if you like juicy, delicious pork. Here's my solution: to compensate for the lack of fat in today's pork, I cook it to a lower internal temperature: 150 to 160 degrees F. While my mom cooked pork to 180 degrees F, that's not necessary—trichinosis is destroyed at 137 degrees F.

JOEY'S

Veal Chops with Portobello Mushrooms

Meat lovers adore this combination of delicate veal and meaty portobello mushrooms. And I find that pounding the veal chops is very therapeutic!

Serves 2

2	**rib veal chops, 12 to 14 ounces each, 1 to 1 ½ inches thick**
¼ cup	**olive oil**
2	**portobello mushrooms, about 4 inches in diameter**
2	**cloves garlic, thinly sliced**
¼ cup	**sherry or red wine**
¼ cup	**Chicken Stock (page 54)**
¼ cup	**chopped fresh basil or Italian parsley**
1 teaspoon	**chopped fresh rosemary (optional)**
	Salt and pepper to taste
1 tablespoon	**butter**

Slice the mushrooms 1/4-inch thick. Place the veal chops between 2 pieces of plastic wrap and pound with a meat mallet to about 1/2-inch thick, being careful not to puncture or tear the veal. Season both sides with salt and pepper.

In a large, heavy skillet (preferably cast-iron), heat the oil to medium high. Add the veal chops and brown for 3 to 5 minutes on each side (for medium rare). Or, if you prefer, grill the veal chops over medium high heat. Remove the chops to serving plates and set aside to rest.

Add the portobello slices to the skillet and sauté until almost cooked through. Add the garlic and sauté for 1 minute. Add the sherry or red wine and ignite with a long-tipped lighter or match, to cook off the alcohol. Add the chicken stock, basil or parsley, rosemary, salt, and pepper to taste. Reduce heat to low and simmer for 5 minutes. Add the butter, stirring until melted. Divide the sauce and mushrooms over the reserved chops and serve.

Veal Chop Milanese

The DeCuffa family comes from Southern Italy, but many of my favorite dishes— like this delicious veal, prepared in the style of Milan—originated in Northern Italy.

Serves 4

4	rib veal chops, 12 to 14-ounces each, 1 to 1 ½ inches thick
¼ cup	flour
3	eggs
¼ cup	chopped fresh Italian parsley
1 tablespoon	grated Romano cheese
	Salt and black pepper to taste
1 ½ cups	Seasoned Bread Crumbs (page 201)
½ cup	Olive Oil Blend (page 198)
2 tablespoons	butter
	Juice of 1 lemon
½ cup	Chicken Stock (page 54)
¼ cup	white wine
¼ cup	grated Asiago cheese
4	lemon wedges, for garnish

Place veal chops between 2 sheets of plastic wrap and pound with a meat mallet to 1/4-inch thickness, being careful not to hit the bone or tear the meat. The pounded chops will be quite large. You may need to cook them one or two at a time, depending on the size of your skillet.

Set 3 shallow dishes in a row. In the first dish, place the flour. In the second, whisk together the eggs, parsley, Romano, salt, and pepper. In the third dish, place the bread crumbs. Press the veal chops into the flour, lightly coating both sides. Dip them into the egg batter, then press both sides in the bread crumbs and set aside.

Preheat the oven to 375 degrees F.

Coat the bottom of a large, heavy skillet with 1/4 inch of oil and heat to medium-high. Add the veal chops and lightly brown on both sides, 3 to 4 minutes. Transfer the chops to a baking dish or sheet pan (You may need two, if the chops are large). Remove any excess bread crumbs from the skillet and return pan to medium-high heat. Add the remaining oil, butter, lemon, chicken stock, and wine. Bring liquid to a boil and allow alcohol to evaporate. Remove the reduced sauce from heat, pour evenly over the veal chops, and sprinkle with the Asiago. Bake for 6 to 8 minutes, until the cheese starts to melt. Transfer the chops to serving plates and top with pan juices. Garnish with lemon wedges.

A Tip from Joey

If you prefer your veal chops less well-done, do not bake them in the oven. Instead, place the baking dish under a preheated broiler until the cheese starts to melt—but be careful not to burn the bread crumbs.

Veal Piccata

The term piccata traditionally implies a tangy sauce of lemon juice, butter, capers, and white wine. At Joey's we add a few extra special ingredients to this classic favorite.

Serves 4

2 pounds	veal cutlets, cut into 4 (8-ounce) pieces, or 8 (4-ounce) pieces
¼ cup	flour
2 tablespoons	Olive Oil Blend (page 198)
2 tablespoons	butter
	Juice of 1 lemon
4	cloves garlic, minced
6	fresh mushrooms, sliced
½ cup	frozen peas
1 teaspoon	Worcestershire sauce
1 tablespoon	Dijon mustard
	Salt and black pepper to taste
½ cup	dry white wine or vermouth
½ cup	Chicken Stock (page 54)
¼ cup	chopped fresh parsley

If the cutlets are too thick, place them between 2 pieces of plastic wrap and gently pound to 1/4-inch thick. Dust the cutlets with an even coating of flour. In a large skillet, heat the oil to medium high. Add the veal and sauté until lightly browned on both sides, about 4 minutes total. Reduce heat to medium. Add the butter, lemon juice, garlic, mushrooms, peas, Worcestershire, mustard, salt, and pepper to taste. Shake the pan over heat to blend ingredients.

Add the wine, increase heat, and return to a boil, stir constantly to prevent sauce from separating. When the sauce is reduced by about half, remove the veal and set aside. Add the chicken stock to skillet, increase heat and bring to a boil. Turn the heat to low and cook until the sauce is reduced to a smooth consistency. Remove from heat. Divide the veal among 4 plates, top with sauce, and garnish with parsley.

Veal Parmigiana

It's easy to confuse Parmigiana with Parmigiano, as in Parmigiano-Reggiano, the world-famous cheese from the Parma region in Central Italy. In this country, Parmigiana has evolved into shorthand for the popular dishes prepared with bread crumbs, tomato sauce, and mozzarella cheese—but no Parmigiano-Reggiano. Go figure.

Serves 4

4	veal leg cutlets, 6 ounces each
1 cup	flour
3	eggs
2 cups	Seasoned Bread Crumbs (page 201)
½ cup	grated Romano cheese
¼ cup	chopped Italian parsley
	Salt and pepper to taste
½ cup	Olive Oil Blend (page 198)
2 cups	Joey's Mother's Sunday Sauce (page 85)
1 cup	grated mozzarella cheese, or 8 slices low-moisture mozzarella
¼ cup	minced fresh Italian parsley

Place the veal between two sheets of plastic wrap and pound with a mallet to 1/4-inch thick, being careful not to puncture or tear veal. Line up 3 shallow bowls. In the first bowl, place the flour. In the second, whisk the eggs. In the third, combine the bread crumbs, Romano, parsley, salt, and pepper. Press the cutlets into the flour, coating both sides, then dip them into the egg. Finally, press both sides of the cutlets into the bread crumb mixture.

Preheat oven to 375 degrees F.

In a large skillet, heat the oil to medium-high. Carefully add the cutlets and pan-fry until evenly browned, 2 to 3 minutes per side. Transfer to a shallow baking dish. Top each cutlet with 1/2 cup Sunday Sauce, then sprinkle or cover evenly with mozzarella. Bake for 10 to 15 minutes, or until the cheese browns and begins to bubble. Remove from oven, sprinkle with parsley, and serve immediately.

Variation: Chicken Parmigiana—replace the veal cutlets with 4 (6-ounce) boneless, skinless chicken breasts, pounded 1/4 to 1/2-inch thick. Proceed as directed for veal.
For a great sandwich, tuck a piece of hot Veal or Chicken Parmigiana into an Italian roll and top with sauce and sliced mozzarella, then bake the sandwich a few minutes to let the mozzarella start to melt. Serve immediately and enjoy!

Stuffed Veal Française

The Italians and the French are always debating about who did what first in the kitchen. This veal may be prepared "in the style of the French," but its ingredients—and inspiration—are pure Italian.

Serves 4

2 pounds	veal cutlets, cut into 8 (4-ounce) pieces
4	thin slices prosciutto
1 cup	grated low-moisture mozzarella
4	broccoli florets, blanched or frozen
½ cup	grated Romano cheese, divided
½ cup	chopped fresh parsley, divided
¼ cup	flour
3	eggs, very cold
	Olive Oil Blend (page 198) to coat bottom of pan to ¼-inch depth

Sauce

¼ pound	butter
½ cup	white wine
¼ cup	fresh lemon juice
1 tablespoon	chopped fresh parsley

For each serving, place 2 cutlets, edge-to-edge, on a clean cutting board. Pound gently with a mallet to fuse into one cutlet, being careful not to tear or puncture veal. Keeping 1-inch at outer edges clear, layer half of each cutlet with prosciutto, mozzarella, and broccoli. Sprinkle with 1 tablespoon each of Romano and parsley. Lightly press ingredients to adhere. Fold the veal in half lengthwise (like a calzone) and lightly pound edges to seal.

Transfer stuffed veal to a plate of flour and gently turn to coat. In a separate, shallow bowl, whisk together the eggs, remaining Romano and parsley. Carefully dip stuffed veal into egg mixture, turning to coat.

In a large skillet over medium-high heat, heat the oil to 375 degrees F. Carefully add the veal and cook for 2 to 3 minutes on each side, turning only once, until golden brown. Carefully remove the veal and drain oil from pan.

Return the veal to skillet and increase heat to medium high. Cut the butter into small pieces and add to pan. Add the lemon juice, white wine, and parsley. Shaking the pan, allow the alcohol to evaporate (or ignite with a long-tipped lighter or match to flambé). Continue to simmer until reduced by about half. The sauce should be velvety smooth. Transfer the stuffed veal to plates, top with sauce, and serve immediately.

Veal Cacciatore

The term cacciatore means "hunter-style" and refers to dishes that are slowly braised or stewed, allowing the ingredients to meet and mingle. By the time they reach the table, all the ingredients are truly simpatico!

Serves 4

1 ½ pounds	**lean veal stew meat, cut into 1 to 2-inch pieces**
½ cup	**flour**
½ to ¾ cup	**Olive Oil Blend (page 198)**
1	**onion, diced**
8	**white mushrooms, sliced ¼-inch thick**
1	**medium carrot, coarsely chopped**
2	**stalks celery, coarsely chopped**
3	**cloves garlic, thinly sliced**
½ cup	**tomato paste**
½ cup	**sherry**
½ cup	**water**
½ cup	**tomato purée**
1 cup	**Chicken or Veal Stock (page 54)**
1 tablespoon	**dried basil**
4 large	**leaves fresh basil, chopped**
	Salt and black pepper to taste
1	**red bell pepper, sliced lengthwise into ¼ to ½-inch-wide strips**
1	**green bell pepper, sliced lengthwise into ¼ to ½-inch-wide strips**
¼ cup	**chopped fresh parsley**
	Grated Romano or Parmigiano-Reggiano cheese, optional

Dust the veal with flour. In the bottom of a large, heavy pot or Dutch oven, add the oil and heat over medium-high heat. Add the veal and sauté, stirring, until meat is lightly browned. Add the onions, mushrooms, carrots, and celery and sauté until softened but not browned, about 3 to 5 minutes. Add the garlic and sauté for 2 minutes. Add the tomato paste and sauté for 2 minutes.

In a separate bowl, combine the sherry and water and stir into the pot. Reduce heat to a simmer and cook for 5 minutes. Add the tomato puree, chicken stock, dried basil, fresh basil and parsley. Season with salt and pepper. Increase heat to medium-high, bring to a boil, then reduce heat to a slow simmer. Cover pan and cook for 30 minutes, stirring occasionally.

Add the bell peppers, cover pan, and continue to simmer for 15 minutes. The dish is done when the peppers are soft and the veal is fork-tender. If necessary, continue to cook at a very slow simmer, stirring occasionally. If the sauce seems too thick, thin with chicken stock, 1/4 cup at a time.

Serve over rice or flat noodles. Garnish with parsley and grated cheese, if desired.

Veal Osso Bucco

At Joey's, this rustic dish is so popular that customers call ahead to reserve their orders. I started making Osso Bucco 25 years ago, when veal shanks were a bargain. They now cost me a fortune, but customers would run me out of town if I took this off the menu.

Serves 4

4	**center-cut veal shanks, about 2 ½ to 3 inches long, 5 to 6 inches in diameter**
⅓ cup	**flour**
1 teaspoon	**salt**
1 teaspoon	**black pepper**
1 teaspoon	**garlic powder**
¼ cup	**Olive Oil Blend (page 198)**
2	**large carrots, peeled, diced**
2	**medium onions, diced**
2	**stalks celery, diced**
4	**cloves garlic, minced**
4 cups	**Veal Stock (page 54) or Beef Stock (page 55)**
4	**whole plum tomatoes, canned**
4	**leaves fresh basil**
1	**sprig of fresh rosemary, leaves only**
½ cup	**sherry or red wine**
¼ cup	**chopped parsley**
4 tablespoons	**grated Parmigiano-Reggiano**

Preheat oven to 375 degrees F.

In a large, shallow bowl, combine the flour, salt, pepper, and garlic powder. Dredge veal shanks in the flour mixture to coat on all sides. In a heavy skillet, heat the oil to medium hot. Add the veal shanks and brown on all sides, turning every 2 or 3 minutes. Remove from skillet and transfer to a roasting pan or large Dutch oven. Add 4 cups of the veal or beef stock and tomatoes. Cover and bake 2 1/2 to 3 hours.

Once the veal shanks are done, remove from the oven and pour off the stock and pan juices into a bowl for later use. Cover the veal shanks and set aside.

Drain most of the oil from skillet that was used for browning the veal shanks, leaving any of the browned flour bits and pieces from the veal shanks along with 1 or 2 tablespoons of oil to sauté the vegetables. Return skillet to stove, and over medium heat, sauté the carrots, onions, and celery for 5 to 8 minutes. Add the minced garlic, basil, and rosemary leaves and sauté for 1 minute. Add sherry or red wine, reduce heat to low, and simmer to reduce, about 5 minutes. Stir in the reserved stock and pan juices that the veal shanks were cooked in. Increase heat, bring to a boil, then reduce heat and simmer for 10 minutes. If the sauce is too thin, mix 1 tablespoon of cornstarch with 1/4 cup of cold water, stir until the sauce thickens into a velvety smooth consistency Add the veal shanks back into the pan and simmer for 10 minutes.

To serve, place one veal shank in a large, shallow soup bowl. Ladle sauce and vegetables equally over each veal shank. Garnish with parsley and grated Parmigiano-Reggiano.

A Tip from Joey

Cooking times are based on veal shanks about 3 inches in diameter. Including meat, the shanks may be 5 to 6 inches in diameter. If yours are much larger, allow extra cooking time.

Chicken

Joey's Chicken Tetrazzini

An American chef created this dish to honor Luisa Tetrazzini, the popular Italian opera star. I find it as soothing as a lullaby.

Serves 4 to 6

1 ½ pounds	**boneless, skinless chicken breast**
¼ cup	**Olive Oil Blend (page 198)**
4	**large white mushrooms, sliced**
½ cup	**sliced roasted red peppers**
1 ½ cups	**heavy cream**
2 tablespoons	**butter**
½ cup	**Chicken Stock (page 54)**
1 cup	**frozen peas, thawed, or fresh, shucked peas, if available**
1 cup plus 2 tablespoons	**grated Asiago cheese**
1 pound	**fettuccine**
¼ cup	**Seasoned Bread Crumbs (page 201)**
	Black pepper to taste

Preheat the oven to 400 degrees F.

Cut the chicken into bite-size pieces. Heat the oil in a large sauté pan over medium heat. Add the chicken pieces and sauté until lightly browned and cooked through, but not dry. Remove the chicken and set aside.

Add the sliced mushrooms to the pan and sauté for 3 to 5 minutes, until soft and lightly browned. Drain the oil and return the chicken to the skillet, along with the roasted peppers, heavy cream, butter, and chicken stock. Bring to a simmer and cook for 5 minutes. Add the peas and 1 cup Asiago, stirring until sauce is creamy and cheese is melted.

While the chicken cooks, prepare the fettuccine according to package directions or pasta instructions on pages 100–101. Drain the fettuccine and transfer to a large casserole. Add half of the chicken mixture and toss lightly with the fettuccine. Spread the remaining chicken mixture over the top and sprinkle with the bread crumbs and remaining Asiago. Bake for about 20 minutes, until the sauce is bubbly and the bread crumbs begin to brown.

Chicken Vermouth

It almost takes longer to read this recipe than to make it—it's that easy. And it's loaded with flavors that just about sing when they get together. For a nice variation, substitute chardonnay for the vermouth, as we do at Joey's at the Thousand Islands Club.

Serves 4

4	**whole boneless, skinless chicken breasts**
¼ cup	**flour**
2 tablespoons	**Olive Oil Blend (page 198)**
3 cloves	**garlic, peeled and minced**
½ cup	**dry vermouth**
8	**white mushrooms, thinly sliced**
	Juice of 1 lemon
2 tablespoons	**butter**
1 tablespoon	**Worcestershire sauce**
2 tablespoons	**Dijon mustard**
	Salt and black pepper to taste
4	**sprigs Italian parsley, chopped**

Thoroughly trim the chicken breasts, separate into halves. Place between two sheets of plastic wrap and pound to about ½-inch thickness. Coat with flour on all sides. In a large sauté pan, heat the oil over medium-high heat. Add the chicken and sauté until lightly brown, about 2 minutes per side. Remove the chicken breasts and set aside, covered with foil to keep warm.

Drain the excess oil, reserving just enough to coat the bottom of the pan. Place the pan over medium-high heat, add the garlic, and sauté for 2 minutes or until soft and fragrant. Add the butter, mushrooms, lemon juice, Dijon mustard, Worcestershire sauce, and parsley. Sauté for 3 minutes, stirring to combine. Season with salt and pepper and remove from heat.

To serve, divide the chicken and mushrooms among four plates and top with the sauce.

Joey's Cannelloni

If I had to reveal my personal favorite on Joey's menu, it would have to be this cannelloni. I'm not alone: customers come back for it, time after time, year after year. My version calls for crêpes rather than pasta—that's the way I learned to make it, and that's the way I love it. I also use both a white sauce and a red sauce, because they balance each other perfectly.

Makes about 8 crêpes

Filling	
3 tablespoons	**olive oil**
1 pound	**ground pork**
1 pound	**boneless, skinless chicken breast, diced**
1 tablespoon	**chicken soup base (see page 200)**
1	**small onion, minced**
1	**small carrot, minced**
¼ cup	**Chicken Stock (page 54)**
1 cup	**fresh chopped spinach**
¼ cup	**grated Romano cheese**
¼ cup	**grated Asiago cheese**
½ pound	**ricotta cheese**
1	**egg**
1 tablespoon	**chopped fresh parsley**
	Salt and black pepper, to taste

In a large skilled, heat the oil over medium-high heat. Add the onion and carrot and sauté until the onion is soft and translucent but not browned, about 5 minutes. Add the pork and cook until lightly browned, about 10 minutes. Add the chicken, chicken base, and chicken stock and stir to combine. Bring to a boil, then reduce the heat to low and simmer, stirring frequently, until the liquid has reduced and the mixture is nearly dry. Add the spinach, turn off the heat, and stir to combine.

Transfer the mixture to a large bowl. Add the Romano and Asiago, stir to combine, and set aside to cool. When cooled to room temperature, add the ricotta, egg, and parsley and blend thoroughly. Season to taste with salt and pepper.

Crêpes	
1 cup	**flour**
2	**eggs**
1 ½ cups	**water**
2 teaspoons	**olive oil**

In a bowl, whisk the flour, eggs, water, and olive oil to batter consistency. Place a crêpe pan or 7-inch sauté pan (nonstick or lightly oiled) over medium-high heat. When the pan is hot, coat the bottom with the crêpe batter. (The thinner the batter, the thinner the crêpes—and thinner is better.) Cook until the crepe starts to bubble on top, then flip carefully with a spatula. Continue to cook until the crêpe slides easily out of the pan. Transfer to a large plate and repeat to make a total of 8 crêpes.

To Assemble

1 ½ cups	**Joey's Mother's Sunday Sauce (page 85)**
1 ½ cups	**Béchamel Sauce (page 201)**
16	**slices low-moisture mozzarella, ⅛-inch thick, or 1 ½ cups shredded mozzarella**

Preheat the oven to 400 degrees F.

Cover the bottom of a large (9 x 13-inch) baking dish with a layer of Sunday Sauce, about 1/4-inch deep.

Spread the crêpes on a clean, dry work surface. At the center of each crêpe, spoon a strip of filling mixture, about 1-inch high. Spread the filling to about 1/2-inch from the crêpe's edge. Fold one end of the crêpe over the filling and roll into a cylinder. Repeat with the remaining crêpes. Carefully transfer the filled cannelloni to the baking dish. Lightly cover each cannelloni with Béchamel Sauce and 2 mozzarella slices (or shredded mozzarella).

Place the dish in the oven and bake until the cheese and Béchamel Sauce begin to brown, about 10 minutes. Serve immediately.

Chicken Saltimbocca

In Italian, saltimbocca means to "leap into the mouth." This popular dish does just that. While saltimbocca is traditionally made with veal, I like to use chicken; in Italy, they often use fresh, young turkey.

Serves 4

4	**whole boneless, skinless chicken breasts**
4	**large, fresh sage leaves (more if leaves are small)**
4	**thin slices prosciutto**
¼ cup	**flour**
4 to 6 tablespoons	**olive oil**
8	**large white mushrooms, sliced**
8 tablespoons	**butter**
1 cup	**white wine**
4	**cloves garlic, peeled and chopped**
¼ cup	**fresh chopped parsley**
¼ cup	**Chicken Stock (page 54)**
1 pound	**fresh baby spinach, washed**
¼ cup (2 ounces)	**chopped prosciutto**

Thoroughly trim the chicken breasts, separate into halves. Place between two sheets of plastic wrap and, using a mallet, pound gently to 1/2-inch thick. Arrange the chicken breasts lengthwise on a clean work surface and center a sage leaf on each breast. On top of the sage, angle 1 slice of prosciutto—the upper half should cover the center of the chicken, and the lower half should extend beyond the chicken and onto the work surface. Lightly pound the prosciutto into the chicken.

Gently flip the chicken breast to the opposite side and fold the extended prosciutto across the center of the chicken. Pound lightly. Place the flour in a shallow dish and carefully coat each chicken breast with flour, making sure both sides are evenly covered.

Place 4 tablespoons of oil in a large skillet and heat to medium high, (375 degrees F). Add the chicken and brown on both sides. If the oil has been absorbed, add another 2 tablespoons and heat briefly. Add the mushrooms and brown lightly. Discard any extra oil. Add the butter to the pan and melt. Add the wine, chicken stock, parsley, and half of the garlic. With a long match or long-tipped lighter, ignite the sauce and allow the alcohol to burn off for a few seconds. Continue to cook until the alcohol has evaporated and the sauce is reduced.

In a separate skillet, heat 2 tablespoons of oil over medium-high heat. Add the spinach, remaining garlic, and chopped prosciutto. Sauté until the spinach is wilted. Divide the spinach mixture among four plates and top each spinach bed with a chicken breast. Pour the sauce over the chicken and serve immediately.

A Tip From Joey

To give this dish a little extra kick, I like to add—while the sauce is reducing—1 teaspoon Dijon mustard, 1 teaspoon Worcestershire sauce, and 1 tablespoon fresh lemon juice.

Joey's Italian Roasted Chicken

This simple recipe delivers incredibly tender chicken with very little effort. Be sure to allow 6 to 8 hours—or better yet, overnight—to let the brine work its magic.

Serves 4

1	**roasting chicken, about 4 to 6-pounds, cut into 8 pieces or 2 each of chicken breasts, thighs, legs, and wings**
4 to 6 tablespoons	**salt**
½ cup	**olive oil**
½ cup	**dry vermouth**
	Juice of 1 lemon
½ cup	**butter**
	Salt and black pepper, to taste
2 tablespoons	**granulated garlic**
1 tablespoon	**paprika**
1	**lemon, sliced**
3	**sprigs fresh rosemary, leaves only**
¼ cup	**minced fresh basil**

Place chicken pieces in a large resealable plastic container. Cover chicken with cold water and 4 to 6 tablespoons of salt. (Ratio is 1 tablespoon salt per pound of chicken). Cover and refrigerate for at least 6 to 8 hours, but no more than 12 hours. Remove the chicken from the brine, rinse well, and pat dry. Return the chicken to refrigerator until ready to cook.

To roast the chicken pieces, preheat the oven to 325 degrees F.

Arrange the chicken pieces, skin-side up, in a large baking pan. Drizzle with the olive oil, vermouth, and lemon juice, in that order. Cut the butter into 16 cubes and tuck between the chicken pieces. Season the chicken with the salt, pepper, garlic powder, and paprika. Arrange a lemon slice over each piece of chicken and sprinkle with rosemary and basil. Bake for about 2 hours until skin is golden brown.

To serve, transfer the chicken to a serving platter. Scrape the pan and pour the juices over chicken. Garnish with additional fresh basil.

A Tip from Joey

To turn this into a one-pot meal, simply peel and slice onions, potatoes, and carrots, and roast them along with the chicken.

Chicken Cacciatore

If your family is like mine, you can keep the peace by tailoring this dish to individual preferences. Instead of cutting a whole chicken into pieces, use only chicken breasts or whatever parts your family prefers. But be sure to use bone-in, skin-on chicken, which has way more flavor.

Serves 4

1	**whole fryer chicken, about 4 to 6 pounds, cut into 8 to 10 pieces**
½ cup plus 2 tablespoons	**Olive Oil Blend (page 198)**
½ cup	**Chicken Stock (page 54)**
½ cup	**coarsely chopped fresh basil**
½ cup	**sherry**
2 cups	**Marinara Sauce (page 86)**
1	**onion, chopped in ½-inch pieces**
1	**clove garlic, peeled and minced**
2 cups	**mushrooms, halved lengthwise**
2	**green bell peppers, cored, seeded, membranes removed, cut in 1-inch strips**
2	**red bell peppers, cored, seeded, membranes removed, cut in 1-inch strips**
	Salt and black pepper, to taste

Preheat the oven to 325 degrees F.

In a large heavy skillet, over medium-high heat, heat 1/2 cup oil, add the chicken pieces, and cook for about 10 minutes, turning to brown evenly. Transfer the chicken to a casserole dish (or Dutch oven) and add the chicken stock, basil, sherry, and Marinara Sauce. Cover and bake for 2 hours. Remove the casserole and set aside. Do not turn off the oven.

In the skillet, heat 2 tablespoons oil over medium heat and add the onions, garlic, mushrooms, and green and red peppers. Sauté until barely soft, about 3 minutes. Transfer the vegetables to the casserole. Return to oven and bake for 10 minutes.

Serve Chicken Cacciatore in shallow bowls or family style on a deep platter. Either way, serve plenty of crusty Italian bread to soak up the sauce!

Chicken Française

When Senator Hillary Rodham Clinton was First Lady, she came to Joey's and asked me for my dinner recommendation. I suggested our elegant Chicken Française. She ordered it, I prepared it, and she loved it. The secret to the puffy crust is to have the eggs very cold and the oil very hot.

Serves 4

4	**whole boneless, skinless chicken breasts**
½ cup	**flour**
¼ cup	**Olive Oil Blend (page 198)**
6	**large eggs, very cold**
2 tablespoons	**chopped fresh parsley**
½ teaspoon	**salt**
½ teaspoon	**ground black pepper**
2 tablespoons	**grated Romano cheese**
½ cup	**flour**
	Juice of 1 lemon
½ cup	**butter, cubed**
1 tablespoon	**chopped fresh Italian parsley**
¼ cup	**white wine**
4	**lemon slices, for garnish**
	Additional chopped parsley, for garnish

Thoroughly trim the chicken breasts, separate into halves. Place between two sheets of plastic wrap and, using a mallet, pound gently to 1/2-inch thick. Set aside. Add 1/4-inch oil to a large sauté pan, place over medium heat, and heat oil to 375 degrees F.

Break the cold eggs into to a shallow bowl and whisk lightly. Add the parsley, salt, pepper, and Romano and whisk to fully incorporate. Spread the flour in a shallow dish. Coat chicken pieces with flour, then dip into the egg batter.

Carefully place the chicken in the hot oil, without crowding. Cook until golden-brown on one side, then turn and cook on the other side. Transfer the chicken to a warm platter. Do not cover, or the coating will become soggy.

Drain the oil and return the pan to medium-high heat. Add the butter and melt. Immediately add the lemon juice and wine and reduce slightly to thicken. Stir in the parsley.

To serve, overlap two pieces of chicken on a plate and spoon lemon sauce over the top. Garnish with chopped parsley.

Joey's Chicken Florentine Braciola

I have been making my famous "Chicken Florentine" rolls for years, mostly for parties. Sliced into rounds and arranged on a platter, they are truly stunning. They're also very versatile and can be served hot or cold as appetizers or entrées.

Serves 4 as a main dish, or 8 as an appetizer

4	whole boneless, skinless chicken breasts
4 cups	oil for frying (preferably peanut oil)
Stuffing	
2 tablespoons	Olive Oil Blend (page 198)
¼ cup	julienned prosciutto or pancetta
1	Spanish onion, minced
2	cloves garlic, minced
1 pound	fresh spinach
¼ cup	julienned sun-dried tomatoes
¼ cup	grated Romano cheese
½ cup	shredded low-moisture mozzarella cheese
¼ cup	Seasoned Bread Crumbs (page 201)
Breading	
½ cup	flour
4	eggs
1 cup	Seasoned Bread Crumbs (page 201)

To make the stuffing, heat the olive oil blend in a sauté pan over medium-high heat. Add the prosciutto (or pancetta) and onion and sauté until lightly browned. Add the garlic and sauté for 2 minutes. Add the spinach and continue to cook until wilted. Remove the pan from the heat and cool to room temperature. When cool, transfer the mixture to a bowl and add the sun-dried tomatoes, Romano, mozzarella, and bread crumbs. Stir to combine and set aside

To make the chicken rolls, thoroughly trim the chicken breasts, separate into halves. Place between two sheets of plastic wrap and, using a mallet, pound as thinly as possible without tearing. Arrange the chicken breasts lengthwise on a flat work surface. Spread two tablespoons of stuffing on each. Starting at its narrowest point, roll each chicken breast as tightly as possible, folding any ragged edges inward.

To bread the chicken, place the flour and bread crumbs on separate plates and whisk the eggs in a shallow bowl. Very carefully coat the chicken rolls in the flour, dip them into the egg batter, and roll in the bread crumbs, gently pressing the crumbs onto the chicken.

To cook the chicken, preheat the oven to 375 degrees F. In a deep-sided sauce pan, heat the frying oil to 375 degrees F. Deep fry the chicken, one roll at a time, until golden brown, about 1 to 2 minutes. Remove and drain on paper towels. Transfer the chicken to a baking dish and bake for 20 minutes. When cooked through, the internal temperature of the chicken rolls should be 165 degrees F. To serve as an entree, place one chicken roll on each plate and top with Béchamel Sauce (page 201).

To serve cold as an appetizer, refrigerate the chicken rolls in an open container for 2 to 3 hours or overnight. Slice the chicken rolls into rounds about ½-inch thick and arrange on a plate or platter with Horseradish Sauce.

A Tip from Joey

A quick-read food thermometer is indispensable in our restaurant kitchen—and a wise investment for the home cook. It tells you when your food is properly cooked and safe to serve. These handy instant-read thermometers are inexpensive and readily available in kitchen supply stores and even supermarkets.

Seafood

Haddock Milanese

When you see the term "Milanese" on the menu, you can usually count on a stylish dish that's punctuated by crunchy, yet buttery, bread crumbs.

Serves 4

2 pounds	haddock fillets
¼ cup	olive oil
½ cup	melted butter
¼ cup	dry white wine
	Juice of 1 lemon
1 cup	Seasoned Bread Crumbs (page 201)
¼ cup	grated Asiago cheese

Preheat oven to 375 degrees F.

Arrange the haddock fillets in a baking dish and drizzle with 2 tablespoons of olive oil, the melted butter, white wine, and lemon juice. Gently lift the haddock so the liquids can seep underneath. In a small bowl, combine the remaining olive oil with the bread crumbs and spoon over the haddock. Sprinkle with the Asiago.

Cover baking dish with aluminum foil and bake for 10 minutes. Remove foil and bake for another 10 minutes or until done. Transfer the haddock to plates and drizzle with the pan juices.

Hot Seafood Antipasto

This flexible recipe works well with all shellfish. Use firm, white-fleshed fish, such as haddock, cod, escolar, or sea bass. Oily, dark-fleshed fish like salmon or mackerel are overpowering.

Serves 4

1 ½ pounds	white-fleshed fish, with skin, cut into 4-ounce pieces
16	littleneck clams in their shells, thoroughly cleaned and rinsed
16	mussels in their shells, thoroughly cleaned and rinsed, beards trimmed
16	medium shrimp, peeled and deveined
¼ cup	olive oil
2 cloves	garlic, minced
¼ cup	water
¼ cup	sherry
¼ cup	chopped fresh basil
2	Roasted Red Peppers (page 29), halved
3 cups	Marinara Sauce (page 86)

In a large, deep skillet or Dutch oven, heat the oil to medium-high. Add the garlic and sauté until softened. Add the basil and peppers and bring to a boil. In a separate bowl, combine the water and sherry. Add to skillet. Add the clams and fish, cover and cook until the clam shells open.

Add the marinara sauce and stir to combine. Add the shrimp and mussels. Bring to a boil, cover, reduce heat, and simmer for 10 minutes or until all mussel shells open. Remove from heat and serve immediately, over linguine if desired.

Honey-Glazed Salmon with Apples

This unlikely but delicious combination comes courtesy of my baby brother, Rick. Like me, he thought he belonged in the dining room with the customers, but once he stepped behind that stove . . .

Serves 4

2 pounds	**salmon fillets, cut into 4 8-ounce pieces—preferably wild**
2	**Red Delicious apples**
4 tablespoons	**butter**
4	**sprigs fresh rosemary**
½ cup	**honey (divided in half)**
¼ cup	**Dijon mustard**
¼ cup	**sour cream**
¼ cup	**mayonnaise**
	Salt and pepper to taste

Preheat oven to 375 degrees F.

Core and cut the apples into eighths. In a medium saucepan, combine the butter, rosemary, 1/4 cup of the honey, and the apples. Cook over medium heat until the apples are soft. Remove from heat and set the apples aside.

In a small bowl, combine the mustard, sour cream, mayonnaise, and remaining 1/4 cup of honey. Arrange the salmon fillets on a greased baking sheet with a rim. Cover the salmon with the mayonnaise mixture. Bake for 12 minutes if you like your salmon medium, plus 3 to 5 minutes more if you prefer it well done. With a spatula, transfer the salmon to serving plates, top with the apples, and garnish with additional rosemary.

A Tip from Joey

I prefer to remove the skin from the salmon so the glaze is in direct contact with the flesh of the fish. To peel the skin, use a knife with a thin, sharp blade. A boning knife is ideal.

Swordfish Pomodoro

With any fish—but especially with swordfish—the operative word is fresh. This is why it's so important to develop a good working relationship with your fishmonger, who will steer you toward the very best and freshest fish.

Serves 4

2 pounds	swordfish, cut into 4 8-ounce pieces, 2 inches thick
½ cup	flour
½ cup	almonds
½ teaspoon	onion powder
½ teaspoon	granulated garlic
¼ cup	Olive Oil Blend (page 198)
1 clove	garlic, minced
4 tablespoons	butter
2	fire-roasted or Italian plum tomatoes, canned, quartered
16	Kalamata olives
4 tablespoons	large capers
1 cup	dry sherry
½ cup	water
	Juice of 1 lemon
4 tablespoons	minced fresh parsley

Preheat oven to 400 degrees F.

Remove (or have your fishmonger remove) bloodline from the swordfish. Rinse the fish but leave damp, so the coating will adhere.

In a food processor, place the flour, almonds, onion powder, and granulated garlic and pulse for about 5 seconds. Transfer mixture to a shallow dish. Evenly coat the swordfish with the flour mixture.

In a large skillet, heat the oil over medium-high heat. Add the swordfish and cook to medium-well. When you press on the swordfish, it will give a little but still feel firm, like the palm of your hand. Transfer the swordfish to a baking dish and bake for 10 minutes.

Meanwhile, in a small pan, heat 2 tablespoons oil over medium-high heat. Add the minced garlic and brown lightly. Add the butter, tomatoes, olives, capers, and lemon juice. In a small bowl, combine the sherry and water, then add it to the tomato mixture. Reduce for 3 to 5 minutes, until alcohol evaporates. Remove the swordfish from oven and transfer to plates. Top fish with sauce and garnish with fresh parsley.

A Tip from Joey

Swordfish steaks have a large surface area, which means they can quickly deteriorate when exposed to air. So buy your swordfish very fresh and serve it as soon as possible, for peak flavor.

Stuffed Calamari

This delicacy is a holiday tradition at Joey's. It takes a little effort, but isn't your family worth it? Use the largest calamari tubes you can find—8 to 10 inches is the ideal size. And be sure to buy domestic calamari—patriotism aside, our calamari is more tender and has more flavor. Filling the calamari tubes can be a little tricky, so recruit a helper to hold the tubes open while you add the stuffing.

Serves 4

3 to 4 tablespoons	Olive Oil Blend (page 198)
1 cup	diced yellow onion
½ cup	diced celery
1 cup	diced red bell pepper
1 cup	diced green bell pepper
1 cup	chopped fresh spinach
1 ½ cups	Seasoned Bread Crumbs (page 201)
¼ cup	grated Romano cheese
1 teaspoon	Old Bay Seasoning or other seafood spice blend
½ pound	shrimp, peeled, deveined, and diced
½ pound	scallops, diced
2 ¼ pounds	large calamari, whole tubes, at least 6 inches long
2 cloves	garlic, minced
½ cup	sherry
½ cup	water
¼ cup	chopped fresh basil
4 cups	Marinara Sauce (page 86)

In a large skillet, heat 2 tablespoons of oil over medium-high heat. Add the onions and celery and sauté for 2 minutes. Add the red and green peppers and sauté for 3 minutes. Add the spinach and sauté until wilted. Add the shrimp and scallops and continue to sauté for 3 minutes. Add the bread crumbs, Romano, and seafood seasoning and stir to combine. Remove from heat and transfer stuffing to a large mixing bowl.

Preheat oven to 375 degrees F.

Inspect the calamari tubes. If there are holes or tears, chop those tubes and use them in the sauce, along with the tentacles. Carefully remove the "fins" from the calamari tubes (they look like little wings). Be gentle: the tubes must be intact to hold the stuffing.

Spoon the stuffing mixture into a pastry bag and pipe into the calamari tubes, filling each tube halfway (This is where an extra set of hands helps. The larger the tube, the easier the job). The calamari will contract during cooking—and burst, if overfilled. Pinch the ends of the tubes together and "pin" each end with a toothpick. With another toothpick, puncture each tube in 4 or 5 places to allow steam to vent during cooking.

Add 1 tablespoon of oil to the skillet and heat over medium-high heat. Add the calamari and sear until lightly browned on both sides, about 3 minutes per side. Remove from skillet and arrange calamari side by side in a baking dish.

Add just enough oil to coat the bottom of the skillet and heat over medium-high heat. Add the garlic and sauté until soft but not browned. Add the reserved calamari tentacles and pieces.

In a separate bowl, combine the sherry and water, add to the skillet, and cook off the alcohol for a few minutes. Stir in the marinara sauce and basil. Bring to a boil. Remove from heat and pour the sauce over the stuffed calamari in the baking dish. Cover the dish tightly with foil and bake for 1½ hours. Remove from oven and allow to rest, covered, for 15 minutes before serving.

As an appetizer, stuffed calamari can be served directly from the baking dish. As a main course, allow three to four small tubes or two larger tubes per person. At Joey's, we serve stuffed calamari over homemade linguine.

Calamari Marinara

Anyone who has cooked calamari knows that you either cook it in a flash or very slowly—there is no middle ground. This dish falls into the slow-cooked category. It's great with just about any pasta, but my preference is linguine.

Serves 4

2 ½ pounds	**calamari, cleaned, preferably domestic**
4 quarts	**water**
2 teaspoons	**salt**
6 cups	**Marinara Sauce (page 86)**
½ teaspoon	**crushed red pepper flakes**
1 pound	**linguine, dried**

In a large stockpot, combine the water and salt and bring to a boil over medium-high heat. Meanwhile, separate the calamari tentacles from the tubes, then cut the tubes into rings about 1-inch wide. Add the tentacles and rings to the boiling water, reduce heat to a slow boil, and cook for 1 ½ to 1 ¾ hours.

In a separate saucepan, bring the marinara sauce to a simmer over medium-low heat. When the calamari pieces are tender, remove them from the boiling water and set aside. Reserve 1 cup of the cooking liquid and add it, ½ cup at a time, to the simmering marinara sauce (be careful not to thin the sauce too much). Stir in the red pepper flakes. Add the cooked calamari, reduce heat to low, and simmer for 30 minutes.

Meanwhile, cook the linguine according to package instructions. Serve the calamari marinara over linguine, with crusty Italian bread to soak up the sauce.

Sea Bass

This is another impressive dish that is deceptively quick and easy to prepare.

Serves 4

4	**sea bass fillets, (8 to 10-ounces each) skin on**
¼ cup	**flour**
1 teaspoon	**salt**
1 teaspoon	**fresh ground black pepper**
1 teaspoon	**granulated garlic**
½ cup	**Olive Oil Blend (page 198)**
4 cloves	**garlic, peeled and sliced thin**
4	**artichokes hearts, canned in water, halved and patted dry**
¼ cup	**sun-dried tomatoes, chopped**
¼ cup	**capers**
	Juice of 1 lemon
4 tablespoons	**butter, cut into 4 pieces**
1 tablespoon	**minced fresh parsley or ½ teaspoon dried**
¼ cup	**white wine or Chicken Stock (page 54)**
Garnishes	
½ cup	**chopped fresh basil**
½ cup	**Crispy Fried Leeks (page 201)**

Preheat oven to 400 degrees F.

In a bowl, mix the flour, salt, pepper and granulated garlic. Dust the sea bass on both sides with flour mix. Coat the bottom of a large sauté pan or skillet with the oil (about 1/4 inch in depth) and heat, over medium-high heat, until the oil is shimmering but not smoking. Add the sea bass, skin-side up, and sauté for 2 to 3 minutes. Turn and sauté the other side for 2 to 3 minutes until golden brown. Transfer the sea bass to a baking dish and bake for 10 to 15 minutes or until done to your preference.

Drain all but 2 tablespoons of oil from the pan. Add the sliced garlic and sauté about 1 minute. Add the artichokes, sun-dried tomatoes, and capers. Sauté for 1 minute and add the lemon juice. Add the wine or chicken stock and deglaze the pan (see Tip page 55). Reduce wine by 75 percent. Add the butter and parsley and stir to combine.

To serve, place one sea bass fillet on each plate and top with one-quarter of the sautéed vegetables. Spoon sauce over each portion and garnish with basil and fried leek garnish.

Lobster Romano

Lobster suggests luxury, yet it's surprisingly simple to prepare. If you want to impress, you can't miss with this glamorous but easy dish.

Serve 4

4	lobster tails in their shells
2	eggs
2 tablespoons	grated Romano cheese
¼ cup	chopped fresh parsley
1 cup	Joey's Seasoned Bread Crumbs (page 201)
4 tablespoons	butter
½ cup	dry white wine
¼ cup	olive oil
	Juice of 2 lemons
¼ cup	grated Asiago cheese

Preheat oven to 400 degrees F.

With a heavy, sharp knife, cut through the top of the lobster shells and split the lobster meat three-quarters of the way through. Spread the shells open, remove the lobster meat, and set aside. Place the shells, with the cut-side down, in a baking dish.

In a bowl, whisk together the eggs, Romano, and parsley. Place the bread crumbs in a shallow dish. Dip the lobster meat into the egg mixture, then coat the lobster with the bread crumbs, pressing to adhere. Carefully transfer the lobster into the inverted shells and return the lobster tails to the baking dish.

In a small saucepan, melt the butter. Stir in the wine, oil, and lemon juice. Bring to a boil and immediately remove from heat. Carefully pour this liquid over the lobster tails, without disturbing the breadcrumbs. Sprinkle with the Asiago and bake uncovered for 10 minutes. Transfer the tails, including their shells, to plates. Pour the liquid from the baking dish over the lobster and serve immediately.

Shrimp and Scallops á la Giussepe

When one of our customers couldn't decide between Shrimp Alfredo and Scallops Marinara, I took the best of both dishes and created this savory combination, which makes welcomed appearances on our specials menu.

Serves 4

1 pound	**large shrimp**
12	**large sea scallops (dry-pack scallops preferred)**
1 tablespoons	**Olive Oil Blend (page 198)**
2 tablespoons	**butter**
1 ½ cups	**heavy cream**
2 cups	**Marinara Sauce (page 86)**
¼ cup	**grated Asiago cheese**
2 tablespoons	**minced fresh parsley**
1 pound	**linguine**

Peel, devein, and butterfly the shrimp. Place a large sauté pan over medium-high heat and coat the bottom with oil. Add the shrimp and scallops and sauté until lightly browned, 3 to 5 minutes. Add the butter and cream, bring to a boil, then reduce heat to a low simmer. Add the marinara sauce and Asiago, and cook, stirring occasionally, for 5 minutes.

Meanwhile, in a stock pot, cook 1 pound of dried linguine according to package directions. Divide the pasta among four plates and cover each portion with shrimp, scallops, and sauce. Garnish with parsley and serve immediately

Shrimp Sambuca

The combination of licorice-flavored Sambuca and shrimp may sound offbeat, but the liqueur gives this dish a slightly sweet and mellow finish. This intriguing recipe is the creation of my long-time chef, Jonathon Blok.

Serves 4

20	**jumbo shrimp, peeled and deveined**
1 tablespoon	**Olive Oil Blend (page 198)**
2 tablespoons	**butter**
2 tablespoons	**chopped garlic**
3 tablespoons	**chopped shallots**
2 teaspoons	**flour**
3 ounces	**Sambuca**
1 cup	**Chicken Stock (page 54)**
1 cup	**heavy cream**
½ cup	**sun-dried tomatoes, thinly sliced**
1 teaspoon	**ground black pepper**
2 teaspoons	**chopped fresh parsley**
1 pound	**linguine, cooked according to package directions**

In a large sauté pan or skillet, heat the oil over medium-high heat. When the oil is hot, add the shrimp and sauté for 5 minutes, stirring constantly so the shrimp cook evenly. Remove the shrimp and set aside.

Add the butter, garlic, and shallots to the skillet and sauté until garlic and shallots are tender, but not browned. Whisk in the flour and thoroughly combine. Add the Sambuca. Using a long-tipped lighter or match, carefully ignite the Sambuca to flambé. Allow the flame to extinguish on its own (it should subside in 10 to 15 seconds).

Return the skillet to medium heat. Add the chicken stock, cream, sun-dried tomatoes, black pepper, and parsley, stirring constantly. Increase heat to medium high, bring to a boil, then reduce heat to low and simmer until sauce starts to thicken. Remove from heat.

To serve, place 5 shrimp on each plate, over linguine or other pasta, if desired. Top with the sauce and serve immediately.

A Tip from Joey

I am a big fan of dry-packed sea scallops, which have less moisture, a firm texture, and more intense flavor. They are increasingly available at large grocery stores and fish markets. If you can't find them, substitute fresh or thawed sea scallops. Before cooking, drain the scallops on paper towels to absorb excess moisture.

Desserts

Tiramisu

With its luscious swirl of Italian flavors and textures, tiramisu holds the title for hottest dessert on Joey's menu. The word tiramisu translates to "lift me up"—in reference, no doubt, to the espresso-fueled perk in every spoonful. If you don't have an espresso machine, swing by your local coffee shop and order 6 ounces of black espresso to go.

Serves 10 to 12

6	**egg yolks**
1 cup	**sugar**
2 cups	**mascarpone cheese**
3 cups	**heavy cream, whipped (see Tip, page 181)**
40	**lady finger cookies, about 4-inches long x 1-inch wide**
¾ cup	**espresso, chilled, or strong black coffee**
¾ cup	**Kahlua, chilled**
2 ounces	**dark chocolate, shaved or finely chopped**
1 ½ teaspoons	**vanilla extract**
	Mint leaves (optional)

In the bottom of a double boiler, bring water to a simmer over medium-high heat.

In the top of the double boiler, whisk together the egg yolks and sugar. Place over the simmering water and continue to whisk, or beat with a handheld electric mixer until stiff ribbons form, about 5 to 8 minutes.

Remove from heat and cool to room temperature. When the mixture has cooled, fold in the mascarpone, blending until no lumps remain. Fold in the whipped cream to just blended with the mascarpone. Do not overfold the whipped cream.

Combine the espresso, Kahlua, and vanilla in a small bowl. Arrange the ladyfingers—in a single layer—on the bottom of a 9 x 13-inch cake pan. You will probably need to cut some of the ladyfingers to fill and fit the pan. Using a tablespoon, spoon the espresso mixture evenly over each lady finger to lightly coat. Spread with half of the mascarpone mixture.

Cover with a second layer of espresso coated lady fingers—arranged in the opposite direction. Cover the lady fingers with the remaining filling.

Sprinkle with the shaved or chopped chocolate. Refrigerate uncovered for at least 2 hours, until the filling is firm.

To serve, slice the tiramisu into 3-inch squares, and if available, garnish with fresh mint leaves.

A Tip from Joey

In my kitchen, whipped cream means real heavy cream, freshly whipped. Forget that ready-to-use stuff that comes in a can (or a tub). Start by chilling a metal mixing bowl and metal beaters in the freezer—for at least half an hour. Be sure the cream is cold as well. When ready to whip, pour the chilled cream into the chilled bowl. Add 1 teaspoon of vanilla extract and 1 tablespoon of granulated white sugar (optional). Using an electric mixer with the chilled beaters, whip the cream on medium-high speed until stiff peaks form. Immediately remove the beaters from the whipped cream—the heat generated by the beaters can quickly turn your cream to butter!

Brosha

After a memorable Sunday dinner in a Tuscan trattoria, we fell under the spell of this creamy, meringue-crusted concoction, sprinkled with vivid red pomegranate seeds. It has the same seductive effect on our customers at Joey's.

Serves 6 to 8

2 cups	heavy cream, chilled
¾ cup	powdered sugar
½ teaspoon	almond extract
2	egg whites
½ cup	sugar
¼ teaspoon	vanilla extract
Pomegranate Sauce	
½ cup	pomegranate juice
2 tablespoons	sugar
½ teaspoon	cornstarch
Garnish	
	Fresh strawberries, raspberries, blueberries, or pomegranate seeds

Preheat oven to 200 degrees F.

In a medium bowl, combine the cream, powdered sugar, and almond extract and beat with an electric mixer, on high speed, until very stiff. Spread the mixture into a shallow baking dish. Cover tightly with plastic wrap and freeze until solid, 4 to 6 hours.

Using an ice cream scoop, form individual balls about 3 inches in diameter (similar to a tennis ball in size) from the frozen cream mixture.

There will be enough mix to make 6 to 8 balls. Transfer to a parchment-lined tray that fits into your freezer. Cover with plastic wrap. Return to freezer until needed.

With an electric mixer on high speed, whip the egg whites until frothy. Gradually add the sugar. Add the vanilla and continue to beat until stiff peaks form. Line a cookie sheet with parchment paper. With a large spoon, scoop and drop meringues onto cookie sheet. Bake for 1 to 2 hours. About halfway through the baking process, lightly pat the center of the meringues down and continue baking until a dry crust forms.

The centers may still be slightly sticky. Remove from oven and cool completely before removing from cookie sheet. Store in an airtight container at room temperature, for up to 1 week.

When ready to serve, crumble the meringues into small, irregular pieces.

Pomegranate sauce: In a saucepan over medium heat, simmer the pomegranate juice until reduced by half. Stir in the sugar and cornstarch and continue to cook until the sauce is smooth and blended.

Remove the brosha from freezer and allow to soften slightly—1 to 2 minutes, until outside appears moist. Press the meringue crumbs onto the outside of the brosha. Drizzle each with pomegranate sauce. Garnish with fresh berries or pomegranate seeds. Serve immediately.

Chocolate Framboise Truffle Tart *from Chef Kathy Bahn*

Trust me, a sliver of this elegant tart goes a long way toward changing your outlook on life

Serves 8

18	lady finger cookies
4 tablespoons	butter, melted
10 ounces	dark chocolate, finely chopped
3 tablespoons	butter
1 cup	heavy cream
¼ cup	Framboise liqueur
1 cup	whipped cream (See Tip page 181)
1 cup	fresh raspberries

In a food processor pulse the lady finger cookies until fine. Transfer to a bowl and mix with melted butter. Press the mixture into the bottom and sides of 9-inch tart pan with a removable bottom.

In the top of a double boiler, over simmering water, combine the chocolate, heavy cream, and butter, stirring occasionally until chocolate is melted. Stir in the Framboise. Pour into prepared tart pan and refrigerate until firm, about 5 hours. Remove sides of pan. Slice tart into 8 pieces and garnish with whipped cream and raspberries.

Lemon Mascarpone Mousse *from Chef Kathy Bahn*

If mascarpone is new to you, be prepared to be impressed. This distant relative of cream cheese is fresh, luscious, and pure Italian. In this recipe, the mascarpone recipe takes ethereal lemon mousse to new heights.

Serves 8

3	whole eggs
3	egg yolks
1 cup	sugar
	Juice of 3 lemons
	Zest of 1 lemon
8 tablespoons	butter, chilled
½ cup	mascarpone cheese
3 cups	heavy cream
16	crisp sugar or waffle cookies, such as Italian "pizzelle" wafers
3 cups	fresh or thawed frozen raspberries
⅓ cup	sugar
1 teaspoon	cornstarch

In the top of a heavy boiler, over simmering water, whisk together the whole eggs, egg yolks, 1 cup sugar, lemon juice, and lemon zest. Continue to whisk until mixture is thickened, about 10 minutes. Remove pan from heat. Cut the chilled butter into small pieces and gradually whisk into warm lemon mixture, blending completely before adding the next piece of butter. After the butter has been blended, add the mascarpone and stir to combine thoroughly. Transfer mixture to a bowl and refrigerate for 1 hour, stirring every 15 minutes.

In a large bowl, whip the cream until very stiff (see Tip page 181). Fold in the chilled lemon mixture. Cover the bowl tightly with plastic wrap and return to refrigerator for 2 hours.

To make the raspberry sauce, puree the berries in a blender or food processor until smooth. Strain through a fine mesh sieve and discard the seeds. In a saucepan, combine the 1/3 cup sugar and cornstarch. Add the berry puree, place the pan over medium heat, and cook until thick and bubbly, about 5 minutes. Cool before serving.

To serve, place a small amount of raspberry sauce on each plate and top with a cookie, then a scoop of mousse. Layer with a second cookie, then another scoop of mousse. Drizzle with raspberry sauce. Serve immediately.

Strawberries DeCuffa

My brother Rick—a performer at heart—created this dessert to celebrate our magnificent Central New York strawberries. Rick makes this tableside—and suddenly every table in the dining room is sending in an order for the fireworks. Inspired by Bananas Foster, it's the ultimate strawberry sundae—for adults only.

Serves 2

2 cups	**fresh strawberries, washed, stems removed, quartered**
2 tablespoons	**Grand Marnier**
1 ¼ ounces	**151 Dark Rum**
1 ¼ ounces	**Crème de Cacao**
¼ cup	**packed light brown sugar**
¼ teaspoon	**ground cinnamon**
1 pint	**premium vanilla ice cream**

Place the butter and brown sugar in a skillet over medium-high heat and stir until melted. Add the rum to the skillet and carefully ignite it with a long match or long-tipped lighter. The rum will burn for about 15 seconds before the flame subsides.

Add the Crème de Cacao, carefully ignite, and allow the flame to burn out. With the skillet still over medium-high heat, add the strawberries and stir to blend. The sauce will start to thicken.

Add the Grand Marnier, carefully ignite, and allow the flame to burn out. Dust with the cinnamon and slowly bring to a boil. Remove skillet from heat and allow the mixture to cool for 3 to 4 minutes.

To serve, place a generous scoop of ice cream (we use vanilla bean) in a shallow bowl. Top with the strawberries and their delectable "sauce."

My Dad's Black and White Cookie

Like many Italians, my father kept no written record of his recipes. So this is my best attempt at recreating the special cookie he created at DeCuffa Brothers Bakery in Utica. I have no doubt my dad is still baking these cookies for the angels—they really are heavenly. Serve with cold milk, and don't forget to raise your glass and toast my dad.

Makes 12 to 16 large cookies

3 cups	**flour**
1 teaspoon	**baking powder**
½ teaspoon	**baking soda**
Pinch	**of salt**
8 tablespoons	**unsalted butter, softened**
1 cup	**sugar**
1	**egg**
2 teaspoons	**vanilla extract**
½ cup	**sour cream**

Heat oven to 350 degrees F.

Coat two large baking sheets with non-stick spray. In a small bowl, combine the flour, baking powder, baking soda, and salt. In a large bowl, beat the butter with an electric mixer on medium speed, scraping down the sides of the bowl 4 to 5 times for 2 to 4 minutes, or until creamy. Slowly add the sugar and continue to beat until blended. Add the vanilla and egg, scraping down the sides of the bowl as needed. Alternately add the flour and sour cream in even batches, mixing until incorporated—but no longer.

With an ice-cream scoop or ¼-cup measure, drop the batter onto cookie sheets, allowing at least 3 inches between cookies. With the palm of your hand, lightly flatten cookies until they are 2 to 3 inches in diameter. Bake for 15 to 18 minutes, until light brown. Rotate the baking sheets if cookies appear to be baking unevenly. Remove from oven and transfer to a wire rack to cool.

White Icing

1 cup	**confectioners' sugar**
¼ cup	**heavy cream**
⅛ teaspoon	**vanilla extract**

Thoroughly blend all ingredients with a whisk.

Black Icing

3 ounces	**semi-sweet chocolate, coarsely chopped**
¼ cup	**heavy cream**
1 tablespoon	**light corn syrup**

Place ingredients in a double boiler over simmering water. Stir until chocolate has melted, and mixture is smooth. Remove from heat, allow to cool for at least 5 minutes until mixture is spreadable.

With a small, angled, metal spatula, spread the white icing over half of each cookie. With a clean spatula, spread the chocolate icing over remaining half. Allow to set at room temperature for 30 to 45 minutes.

Store the cookies between layers of wax paper in an airtight container.

Joey's Classic New York Cheesecake

Italians have been making ricotta-based cakes since Roman times, but when it comes to cheesecake, I side with the home team. This New York City classic has earned all-star status at Joey's.

Serves 12

Crust	
2 cups	**graham cracker crumbs**
½ cup	**light brown sugar**
8 tablespoons (4 ounces)	**butter, melted**
	Pinch of ground cinnamon
	Nonstick baking spray

Filling	
2 pounds	**cream cheese (regular or light)**
2 ½ cups	**sugar**
1 tablespoon	**vanilla extract**
1 cup	**sour cream**
6	**eggs**

Preheat oven to 325 degrees F.

Line the bottom of a 10 x 3-inch springform pan with parchment paper. In a small bowl, thoroughly combine the graham cracker crumbs, brown sugar, melted butter, and cinnamon. Press the crumb mixture into the bottom of the springform pan, then spray the inner edges of the pan with nonstick spray.

With a heavy-duty electric mixer on medium speed, blend together the cream cheese, sugar, and vanilla extract. Scraping down the mixture from sides of bowl, continue to beat for several minutes, until creamy but not soupy. Add the sour cream and blend. Add the eggs, 2 at a time, blending thoroughly after each addition. Pour the filling into springform pan and smooth top. Filling should reach to about 1/2-inch below pan rim. Do not overfill!

To create steam in the oven—and keep the cheesecake moist while baking—place 2 cups of water in a baking pan and place on the oven rack below the cheesecake. If the water evaporates during the baking process, add more hot water, 1/2 cup at a time.

Bake the cheesecake for 1 1/2 to 2 hours, until the center is firm and no longer jiggles. Remove the cheesecake from oven and cool to room temperature, about 2 hours. Refrigerate the cake for at least 12 hours before serving.

To serve, carefully remove the sides of the springform pan. Slice the cheesecake into 12 wedges by running a knife under hot water, wiping it dry and repeating the process after each slice.

This cheesecake is wonderful by itself—or garnished with fresh fruit, fruit sauce, or whipped cream.

Biscotti

At Joey's, we serve these rustic—and quintessentially Italian—cookies with special coffees, but we also use them, crushed, in other desserts. For a quick, crunchy ice-cream topping, try crumbling your own biscotti*

Makes about 24 biscotti

2 cups	flour
½ teaspoon	baking soda
¼ teaspoon	salt
¼ teaspoon	ground cinnamon
1 cup	hazelnuts, coarsely chopped
2	large eggs
¾ cup	sugar
¼ cup	amaretto liqueur
½ teaspoon	vanilla extract

Preheat oven to 325 degrees F.

Line 2 cookie sheets with parchment paper. In a large bowl, sift together the flour, baking soda, salt, and cinnamon. Stir in the hazelnuts.

In separate bowl, combine the eggs, sugar, amaretto, and vanilla. Add the flour mixture to the wet mixture and combine thoroughly with a spatula. (The dough will be sticky.)

Using your hands, scoop half of the dough onto each of the parchment lined-baking sheets. Form the dough into a rectangular log about 1-inch thick. Bake for 40 minutes, until light, golden brown. Remove from the oven and cool the biscotti on the baking sheets, leaving the oven temperature at 325 degrees F.

When logs are cool, cut crosswise into 1-inch slices. Stand slices on baking sheet and bake for another 10 minutes. Transfer to wire racks to cool completely. Store in an airtight glass or plastic container.

Variation: To make biscotti crumbs for pie crust, drop whole biscotti into a food processor or blender and grind to desired consistency and quantity of biscotti crumbs

Pumpkin Cheesecake with Pecan Graham Cracker Crust, White Chocolate Ganache and Caramel Sauce *from Chef Kathy Bahn*

Our customers at Joey's crave this seasonal variation on a New York classic. A lot of folks serve it for Thanksgiving, instead of pumpkin pie

Serves 12

Crust

1 recipe	Joey's Classic New York Cheesecake Crust (page 190)
½ cup	raw, unsalted pecans, finely chopped

Cheesecake

1 ½ pounds	cream cheese, cold
1½ cups	sugar
1 ½ teaspoons	vanilla extract
1 ½ teaspoons	ground cinnamon
1 teaspoon	ground ginger
	Dash of nutmeg
½ teaspoon	salt
1 ½ cups	unseasoned pumpkin purée, canned or frozen (thawed)
5	eggs cracked into a separate bowl
3 tablespoons	flour
3 tablespoons	unsalted butter, melted

White Chocolate Ganache

½ cup	heavy cream
1 tablespoon	sugar
6 ounces	white chocolate, finely chopped

Caramel Sauce

1 cup	store bought caramel sauce in a squeeze bottle

Preheat oven to 325 degrees F.

Line the bottom of a 10 x 3-inch springform pan with parchment paper. In a small bowl, thoroughly combine the graham cracker crumbs, brown sugar, melted butter, and cinnamon. Press the crumb mixture into the bottom of the springform pan, then spray the inner edges of the pan with nonstick spray.

Using a large bowl and electric mixer set at medium speed, beat the cream cheese, sugar, vanilla, salt, and spices for about 5 minutes, until very smooth. Scrape down sides of bowl and clear the beaters frequently to break up any lumps. Reduce the mixer speed to low, add the pumpkin puree, and blend for about 1 minute, scraping down the sides of the bowl. Add the eggs and mix just until blended. Add the melted butter and flour, blend for 30 seconds. Pour the filling into the prepared crust.

To create steam in the oven—and keep the cheesecake moist while baking—place 2 cups of hot water in a baking pan and place on the oven rack below the cheesecake. If the water evaporates during the baking process, add more water, 1/2 cup at a time.

Bake the cheesecake for 1 1/2 to 2 hours—oven temperatures vary so check with a baking thermometer. Be gentle when opening or closing the oven door: shaking the pan or slamming the oven door can cause the cheesecake to crack. The cheesecake is done when center doesn't jiggle, and the top has risen slightly. Remove from oven and cool on a wire rack.

To make the ganache: In the bottom of a double boiler, bring water to a simmer over medium heat. Place all ingredients in the top of the double boiler and cook, stirring, over simmering water, until melted and blended. Remove from heat.

Carefully remove the sides of the cheesecake pan. Pour 1/2 of the ganache over the top of the cooled cheesecake, tipping the cake top for even coverage. Transfer the remaining white chocolate mixture to a stainless steel bowl and place in a shallow ice bath (2 cups cold water, 2 cups ice). Cool the mixture until it reaches the consistency of frosting, about 2 minutes. With a narrow-blade spatula, spread the thickened white chocolate mixture evenly around the sides of the cheesecake. Press the chopped pecans into the sides of the cheesecake.

Refrigerate for 30 minutes. Remove the cheesecake from refrigerator and drizzle the top with caramel sauce, creating a grid or swirl pattern. Return the cheesecake to refrigerator for 30 minutes before serving. To serve, carefully remove the sides of the springform pan. Slice the cheesecake into 12 wedges by running a knife under hot water, wiping it dry and repeating the process after each slice. Garnish with additional caramel sauce, toasted, chopped pecans, and whipped cream, if desired.

Apple-Cranberry Tart with Port Wine Glaze

I have no clue why New York City is called the Big Apple. But I know that Central New York has the best apples I've ever tasted. At Joey's, our customers love this combination of crisp local apples and sweet-tart cranberries—another original creation from our pastry chef, Kathy Bahn.

Serves 8

Crust

3 cups	flour
1 cup	cold shortening, preferably Crisco
1 tablespoon	butter, cold
½ cup	cold water

In a mixing bowl, combine the flour, shortening, and butter. Using your hands, a pastry cutter or fork, cut the shortening into the flour, until the mixture resembles fine crumbs. Add the water and gently knead with your hands just until the dough holds together and forms a ball. (Overworking the dough toughens the crust.) Divide the dough into two pieces: 2/3 for the bottom crust and 1/3 for the lattice top.

Filling

5	crisp, tart apples, such as Granny Smith peeled, cored, and sliced in ⅛-inch wedges
1 cup	dried sweetened cranberries
1 ½ teaspoons	ground cinnamon
¼ cup	flour
¼ cup	sugar
¼ cup	light brown sugar

In a small bowl, stir together the flour, both sugars, and cinnamon. In a large mixing bowl, combine the apples and dried cranberries. Sprinkle the fruit with the dry ingredients and stir to combine.

Cobbler Topping

½ cup	flour
½ cup	light brown sugar
4 tablespoons (2 ounces)	butter, softened
½ teaspoon	ground cinnamon

In a bowl, thoroughly mix all ingredients with a fork or by hand—the texture should be crumbly.

Egg Wash

1	egg
1 tablespoon	cold water
1 tablespoon	sugar

In a small bowl, mix the egg and water with a fork until blended. Set aside sugar.

Port Wine Glaze

1/4 cup	sugar
1/2 cup	water
3/4 cup	port, such as Ruby Red, preferred for its berry, spicy, autumn flavors
2 cups	apple juice
1/8 teaspoon	ground ginger
1/8 teaspoon	ground cinnamon
3 tablespoons	cold water
1 tablespoon	cornstarch

In a saucepan, combine the sugar and water and bring to boil on medium high heat, stirring occasionally until the mixture turns golden brown. Add the port, and simmer until reduced by 2/3. Add the apple juice, ginger, and cinnamon. Return to a simmer, and cook, stirring occasionally, until reduced by 1/2, about 10 to 15 minutes.

In a small bowl, thoroughly blend the cold water and cornstarch. Slowly add to the port mixture, stirring constantly to thicken. Remove from heat and place pan in an ice bath (2 cups cold water and 2 cups ice) to cool glaze.

To make the tart: Preheat oven to 325 degrees F.

On a lightly floured surface, roll the larger ball of dough into a circle about 1/8-inch thick. The circle should be large enough to cover the bottom and sides of a 9-inch tart pan with a removable bottom. Carefully place the crust in the pan, folding any overhanging dough to the inside. Pour the filling into the crust. Spoon the cobbler topping evenly over the filling.

For the lattice crust, roll the second piece of dough into a circle about 1/8-inch deep and 9 inches in diameter. Cut the circle into strips about 1/2 inch in width. Weave the strips into a lattice pattern on top of the filling. Using a pastry brush, carefully brush the strips with egg wash, then sprinkle with 1 tablespoon sugar.

Bake for 1 1/2 hours. Remove tart from oven and cool for 30 minutes before serving.

This tart is delicious served warm or cold. To serve warm, allow the tart to cool for 20 to 30 minutes before cutting. Drizzle each serving with the port wine glaze and top with whipped cream (see Tip page 181) or vanilla ice cream.

Pantry

Joey's Pantry

If you grew up—as I grew up—around Italian cooking, you probably learned about ingredients by osmosis. No one formally lectured you or—heaven forbid!—wrote anything down. They just used the best ingredients available—a resourceful mix of homegrown, imported and domestic—and those tastes set the standard for the rest of your life.

Today, it's not so simple. There are entire supermarket aisles of Italian or Italian-inspired ingredients. The priciest version of a product is often not necessary, or even appropriate. Authentic balsamic vinegar, for example, would be wasted in a salad dressing. At $50 an ounce, Italians reserve this prized liquid for tasting only, from the tip of a silver spoon, or drizzling over perfect, ripe strawberries. Even when excellent ingredients are affordable and widely available, they are not necessarily suitable. Fresh mozzarella—a memorable treat in a cool, summer salad—disintegrates under high heat. No point in heaping it on oven-bound casseroles or other dishes that call for long baking times.

My purpose, in this pantry, is not to write an encyclopedia of Italian ingredients. I'm simply listing a few core recipes and sharing basic guidelines about the products I prefer (which are often the products my Italian-tutored mother preferred). Feel free to use what your mother or grandmother used. Or let me know if you disagree with my choices. There's nothing we Italians like better than a lively argument, especially when the topic is Italian cooking!

Olive Oil and Olive Oil Blend

Have you ever noticed that foods that grow together go together? The simple concept of common ground explains why olive oil brings out the best in other Italian produce like tomatoes, basil, and garlic. Different regions of Italy produce distinct olive oils, from delicate to outright spicy. As with wine, it's a matter of personal preference. My only advice is to use cold-pressed, extra virgin olive oil for salad dressings and dipping sauces. This grade of olive oil is extracted, without heat, from the first pressing of the olives, and the flavors are fresh and vibrant.

When cooking at low to medium temperatures, I use pure olive oil from Italy. While it's produced with heat, to increase yield, it still tastes mild and pleasant. When cooking at high heat, I use Olive Oil Blend, a mix of 10 percent olive oil and 90 percent vegetable oil (which has a higher smoke point). You can buy it already blended (sold as Blended Oil) or mix it yourself, using one part olive oil to nine parts vegetable oil.

Balsamic Vinegar

When Joey's customers order oil and vinegar with their salads, we send out balsamic vinegar. No question, balsamic vinegar is seductive. The finest balsamic is made by hand, usually at home, in Modena, Italy. As the vinegar becomes more concentrated and complex in taste, it is transferred into wooden barrels that are progressively smaller—and so prized they are often included in a woman's dowry. It takes 12 years and priceless TLC to age authentic balsamic vinegar. Most of what we consume in the U.S. has a less romantic pedigree. It's commercially produced, but I still love its edgy sweetness. When I want the flavor of balsamic vinegar, but I don't want to alter the color of the other ingredients (such as my Calamari Salad page 43), I use white balsamic vinegar, which is clear and comparable in taste.

Tomatoes

My father's roots are in Southern Italy, where tomatoes thrive in the sunny climate and star in the cuisine. But the tomato is not native to Italy. In the 1600s, it was carried back to Europe from "the New World" and embraced by the discerning but thrifty Italians. When they eventually migrated to the United States, they carefully packed their tomato seeds—talk about coming full circle!

In my opinion, fresh local tomatoes are the essence of summer and perfect for fresh tomato sauce, which cooks in a flash. When I make my marinara sauce, I use canned San Marzano tomatoes from Italy—a little pricey, but worth every penny. For my mother's Sunday sauce, the signature sauce at Joey's, I use high quality crushed California tomatoes in heavy puree. They are slightly more acidic than the Italian imports, but these hearty domestic tomatoes stand up better to several hours on the stove.

Sauce

We first bottled Joey's tomato sauce 15 years ago, but the story goes back 50 years, to when I was a baby in Utica. Our upstairs neighbors were the Alesias. Betty Alesia was my mother's best friend, and her son Rick became my best friend—our moms tell us we used to play in the crib together. Both Betty and my mother lost their husbands way too early, so they stuck together and they raised all their kids (and there were a lot of us!) like one big family. Fast forward about 40 years: I'm at Joey's. Rick Alesia is on the retail end of the food business. We are still best friends. Rick, who's a great cook himself, suggests that we bottle and sell Joey's tomato sauce. Suddenly we're trying to convert my recipes from 2-gallon to 500-gallon batches. I didn't think we could maintain any kind of quality at that volume. But by sticking to my mantra about top-shelf ingredients and no shortcuts, we came up with a tasty trio of Joey's sauces; Marinara, Cacciatore and Fra Diavolo. The best news is that—despite those warnings about not mixing business with friendship—Rick and I are still best friends.

Joey's sauces can be purchased at Joey's restaurants and they are also available at several Central New York grocers including Wegman's and P&C Markets. To order by phone call Joey's at 315-432-0315.

Granulated Garlic

In the process of translating my unwritten restaurant recipes into recipes for the home kitchen, the most-debated ingredient has been granulated garlic. Not to be confused with garlic powder, granulated garlic is dehydrated garlic ground to a sugar-like consistency and will be a darker brown than garlic powder. I use it when I want the gusto but not the sharper bite of fresh garlic. One-quarter teaspoon of granulated garlic is equal to 1 clove of garlic.

Garlic powder, which I don't recommend, is also made from dehydrated garlic but is finer in texture, often made with filler, and the flavor is not as satisfying as granulated garlic.

While garlic powder is easy to find in the spice section of your supermarket, you may have to dig a bit for granulated garlic. Check the Italian imports aisle. Look for clear packaging so that you can see the consistency of the granulated garlic, which should look like granulated sugar, or even slightly coarser. Let the texture be your guide as there are some products labeled garlic powder that are actually granulated and vice versa. I am still a fan of fresh garlic but prefer granulated garlic for certain recipes.

Fresh Mozzarella

Our American infatuation with fresh mozzarella is certainly justified. Its softer (but still resilient) texture and sweet, milky taste provide a wonderful contrast to more intense Italian flavors. Fresh mozzarella (even better, mozzarella di bufala) makes a great addition to a summer salad or antipasto platter. But fresh mozzarella, packed in water, is highly perishable. It disintegrates under high heat, and browns or burns too quickly to use in some recipes. For everyday melting—and grating—I recommend whole-milk, low-moisture mozzarella.

Stocks and Bases

I feel strongly about the superiority of homemade stock. It is almost effortless to make (the heat of your stove does most of the work), and it adds deep, layered flavor to soups, stews, and sauces. If you don't have homemade stock on hand, I recommend that you substitute a concentrated soup base that's been mixed with water. Excellent soup bases—in chicken, beef, and a variety of flavors—are readily available in supermarkets. I find these products preferable to canned broths and vastly superior to bouillon cubes, which are packed with salt and faintly flavored, at best. Even when you're using homemade stock, I often suggest adding a dash of concentrated soup base, for an extra punch of flavor.

Following are a few core recipes you will refer to again and again in my recipes.

Garlic Butter

At Joey's we go through tubs of garlic butter every day. This simple recipes will become a favorite in your kitchen. Use on bread, toss with pasta, or try on a grilled steak.

Makes about 1 ½ cups

1 cup	**salted butter, softened or whipped salted butter**
⅛ cup	**fresh garlic cloves, minced**
¼ cup	**fresh Italian parsley, minced**

Using a mixer or food processor, slowly mix or pulse the butter and garlic to combine. Stir in parsley until just blended. (Too much mixing will result in an unappetizing green butter.)

Place in a sealable container, refrigerate and use within 2 weeks. For another serving option, chill the butter and roll it into a "rope" about 1-inch thick. Wrap in plastic wrap and chill or freeze. Then, cut butter into little rounds for use on meat, poultry, fish, or vegetables.

A Tip from Joey

Try roasting the garlic before mixing it in with the butter for a savory taste (page 26).

Joey's Seasoned Breadcrumbs

Makes about 3 cups

1	large loaf Italian bread
3 tablespoons	dried basil
2 teaspoons	salt
2 teaspoons	ground black pepper
¼ cup	grated Romano cheese
¼ cup	dried parsley flakes
3 tablespoons	garlic powder

Preheat oven to 375 degrees F.

Slice bread, spread out on a large baking sheet, and toast lightly until it is crisp and crumbly, but not dark. Set bread aside to cool. In a food processor fitted with a steel blade, grind toasted bread into fine crumbs. In a large mixing bowl, combine bread crumbs with remaining ingredients. Store in a dry, airtight container in a cool, dry place. For best results, use within one week because like bread, breadcrumbs will become stale.

Béchamel Sauce, aka White Sauce

Makes about 1 ½ cups

3 tablespoons	butter
3 tablespoons	flour
1 cup	heavy cream, cold
¾ cup	Chicken Stock (page 54)
	Salt and pepper, to taste
	Dash of nutmeg

In a saucepan, melt the butter over medium heat. Whisk in the flour and continue to stir for 2 to 3 minutes to make a paste, or roux.

Add the cream, chicken stock, salt, pepper, and nutmeg. Whisk constantly until sauce starts to bubble. Continue to whisk until sauce is creamy and thick enough to coat a spoon. Remove the pan from heat and set aside to cool.

Crispy Fried Leeks

Makes about ½ cup

1	medium leek
2 tablespoons	flour
	Salt and ground black pepper
½ cup	Olive oil

Halve leek lengthwise using white and light green parts. Slice into very thin 2-inch long strips

Toss leeks, flour, and a pinch each of salt and pepper together in a bowl. In a 12-inch skillet heat the oil until shimmering. Add half of the sliced leeks and fry, stirring often, until golden brown, about 6 minutes. Using a slotted spoon, transfer leeks to a plate lined with paper towels. Season with salt and pepper. Repeat with remaining leeks. Serve as a garnish for fish, soup or to add a special touch to a salad.

(L–R) Rick Zaborny, Joey, Jonathon Blok, and Kathy Bahn

Index

Words in italics indicate a recipe, page numbers in italics indicate a photograph.

K

L

M

O

P

R

S

T

U

V

W

Joey's cookbook team

(L-R) Holly Scherzi, Janice DeCuffa, Jim Scherzi, Joey, and Denise Harrigan

Joey's and Pronto Joey's

6594 Thompson Road North @ Carrier Circle
Syracuse, NY 13206
Joey's: 315.432.0315
Pronto Joey's: 315.432.0620
Fax for both restaurants: 315.434.9950
Joey's Catering: 315.410.1753 or 315.432.0315

Joey's at the Thousand Islands Club

Open seasonally from May to September
21952 Club Road
Wellesley Island, NY 13640
Call year round: 315.482.9999
Call anytime for wedding, banquet, and all catering services

For information on all three Joey's Restaurants
please visit: www.JoeysItalianRestaurant.com